A More Perfect Torah

CRITICAL STUDIES IN THE HEBREW BIBLE

Edited by

Anselm C. Hagedorn
*Humboldt
Universität zu Berlin*

Nathan MacDonald
University of Cambridge

Stuart Weeks
Durham University

A More Perfect Torah

At the Intersection of Philology and Hermeneutics in Deuteronomy and the Temple Scroll

For Andrew,
Congratulations on the
beautiful edition of the Temple
Scroll — and on your new
edition in progress. I think you
will find material here also of interest —
and you helped a great deal way
back in 2001 with the
original publication
of ch. 1 — Thank you.

BERNARD M. LEVINSON

Best wishes,
Bernard Levinson
17 Aug 2015

Winona Lake, Indiana
EISENBRAUNS
2013

Library of Congress Cataloging-in-Publication Data

Levinson, Bernard M. (Bernard Malcolm)
A more perfect Torah : at the intersection of philology and hermeneutics
   in Deuteronomy and the Temple scroll / Bernard M. Levinson.
     pages cm. — (Critical studies in the Hebrew Bible ; number 1)
   Includes bibliographical references and indexes.
   ISBN 978-1-57506-259-4 (pbk. : alk. paper)
   1. Jewish law—Interpretation and construction.   2. Hebrew
language—Syntax.   3. Bible. O.T. Deuteronomy—Criticism,
interpretation, etc.   4. Dead Sea scrolls.   5. Vows (Jewish law)
6. Rabbinical literature—History and criticism.   I. Title.
   BM521.L465   2013
   222′.1506—dc23
                                                    2012045738

In Memoriam

THERESA ACKERMAN BERMAN

October 8, 1912 – November 8, 2012

פִּיהָ פָּתְחָה בְחָכְמָה וְתוֹרַת־חֶסֶד עַל־לְשׁוֹנָהּ:

She opens her mouth with wisdom,
And the teaching of kindness is on her tongue.
(Proverbs 31:26)

Contents

List of Figures

Preface

This book brings together two studies that investigate the relationship between the compositional history of the biblical text and its reception history at Qumran and in rabbinic literature. The book equally seeks to bring together historical linguistics (with a focus on the syntax of conditional clauses in biblical law) with the study of hermeneutics (in this case, the way the Pentateuch was interpreted during the Second Temple period). Each study examines the relation between language, text, and scribal practice in the writing, transmission, and reception of the Pentateuch. My goal is to complicate the relationship between "Scripture" and "Rewritten Scripture" and to show the connections between the two categories.

Part I is entitled "Revelation Regained: The Hermeneutics of כי and אם in the Temple Scroll." Co-written with Molly M. Zahn just over a decade ago, it is republished here in lightly revised and updated form with her kind agreement.[1] This study examines the frequent replacement of conditional כי with אם in the Temple Scroll and argues that a new conceptual model is necessary to explain the phenomenon accurately. We argue that historical linguistics alone does not explain the distribution of the two conditionals in the Temple Scroll or account for the conditions that govern the replacement of כי by אם. In order to explain the evidence, it is necessary to take a much broader look at the phenomenon of conditional markers in Sumero-Akkadian law and Northwest Semitic (especially the Ugaritic hippiatric corpus). We demonstrate the distinctive systems for marking a protasis that operate in each of the three legal collections of the Pentateuch (the Covenant Code, Deuteronomy, and the Holiness Code). The author of the Temple Scroll must have recognized these

---

1. Bernard M. Levinson and Molly M. Zahn, "Revelation Regained: The Hermeneutics of כי and אם in the Temple Scroll," *DSD* 9 (2002) 295–346. The present version takes into account new critical editions of the Temple Scroll (see p. 3 n. 2) and more-recent secondary literature. I have clarified the analysis of the morphosyntax of cuneiform law and adjusted some formulations and translations throughout. Footnote numbering intentionally remains consistent, except that p. 32 n. 84, which makes a bridge to part 2, is new; accordingly, footnote numbers thereafter differ by one.

different systems implicitly and, at key points, sought to align them and to introduce greater consistency in their use as part of his overall project. This hypothesis was confirmed by investigating the system of paragraph markers in the Temple Scroll, where we could demonstrate a clear connection between conditional כי and the beginning of a new literary unit (appendix 2 provides the evidentiary base for our arguments). The most gratifying part of the project was the way the data mutually reinforced one another. The data from philology (syntax and historical linguistics) and the argument from hermeneutics (the way the Temple Scroll author rewrote and reorganized sequences of biblical law) were consistent both with one another and with the scribal practices employed in writing the manuscript.

Part 2 is entitled "Reception History as a Window into Composition History: Deuteronomy's Law of Vows as Reflected in Qoheleth and the Temple Scroll." It represents new work, and here I am the sole author. This study, which builds on part 1, case 4, closely examines the syntax and content of the law of vows in Deut 23:22–24. The argument is that the law contains a previously unrecognized textual disruption. The interpretive issue arises from the law's syntax (its sequence of conditional כיs, which I believe to be problematic), as well as from its content (its sequence of thought). In order to confirm the hypothesis of a textual disruption, I found it necessary to work on two levels of analysis. Semantically, I investigated the use of conditional כי throughout the legal corpus of Deuteronomy in order to understand its function and distribution (see appendix 3). Exegetically, I turned to the history of the reception and interpretation of Deuteronomy's law of vows in antiquity, examining how it was read and responded to during the Second Temple period, both within the Bible and at Qumran, as well as in rabbinic literature (specifically, Qoh 5:4–7, 11QTemple 53:11–14, Numbers 20, and *Sipre Deuteronomy*). Both Qoheleth and the Temple Scroll directly respond to Deuteronomy's law of vows at the points that I identified as problematic. Each author "corrects" the text, but each does so in different ways. The two mutually independent revisions thus reinforce the argument for an interpolation; this textual disturbance was already implicitly sensed in antiquity. Further evidence for the hypothesis is then provided by the reception of the law of vows in Numbers 20, the set of priestly rules governing the annulment of vows and oaths. I argue that the text witnesses an earlier version of Deuteronomy's law of vows before the textual disruption took place. Finally, I examine how the rabbinic legal exegesis of *Sipre Deuteronomy*, in responding to the law of vows, was unable to reconcile the inconsistent guidelines that resulted from the textual disruption.

In part 2, just as with part 1, I seek to make a methodological contribution. My argument is that the history of the reception and interpretation of the Bible in the Second Temple period offers a window into the compositional history of the biblical text. Analysis of the exegetical reworking of the Bible in the Dead Sea Scrolls and in rabbinic literature can provide a valuable critical tool for a more acute understanding of the process of composition of the biblical text. The logic of placing part 1 first in the sequence of presentation is therefore not only because it was written first. By beginning with the Temple Scroll and then working back to the more detailed study of the biblical text (in part 2), I sought to implement the book's larger intellectual project: to show the relevance of reception history for understanding composition history.

It was very gratifying to learn that this manuscript was accepted to inaugurate the new Eisenbrauns series Critical Studies in the Hebrew Bible. Anyone who recalls the helpful series Fortress Guides to Biblical Scholarship, with its valuable and short guides will welcome the initiative by Anselm Hagedorn, Nathan MacDonald, and Stuart Weeks, with support from Eisenbrauns, to develop a comparable new series of short, subject-specific monographs.[2] I am grateful to the series editors for obtaining two detailed, constructive referee's reports on my manuscript, which helped me revise and improve it. Responsibility for any errors remains, of course, my own. I want to thank Jim Eisenbraun for his encouragement, professionalism, and immense patience; as well as Beverly McCoy for her precision as copy editor and commitment to clear writing. I take this opportunity to thank Mike Bartos, my research assistant, who is currently completing his Ph.D. at McMaster University, for his engaged assistance and contributions to this project, going back now over six years. J. P. Kang provided expert help with conversion to Unicode fonts and assistance with some of the diagrams. I am grateful to the University of Minnesota's Imagine Fund for the Arts and Humanities for generously supporting faculty research. My deepest debt of thanks goes to Hanne Løland Levinson, to whom, with love, I have made the most significant vow of my life, for her careful reading and valuable suggestions.

This volume was originally intended to commemorate the 100th birthday of Theresa Ackerman Berman who with her husband, Nathan,

---

2. One of my favorites was Norman C. Habel, *Literary Criticism of the Old Testament* (Guides to Biblical Scholarship; Philadelphia: Fortress, 1971).

son Lyle, and daughter-in-law Janis founded the Berman Family Chair of Jewish Studies and Hebrew Bible at the University of Minnesota, a position that I am honored to hold. Theresa was graduated from the University nearly eight decades ago. She took an active interest in supporting undergraduate education across the curriculum, including the fine arts, Jewish Studies, library resources, and Minnesota history. I greatly admired her sense of civic duty and her values. One month after celebrating her centennial birthday, she passed away; this monograph therefore commemorates Theresa in memoriam.

—*B. M. L.*
Israel Institute for Advanced Studies, Jerusalem
May 7, 2013

Abbreviations

General

b.	*Babli*: tractate in the Babylonian Talmud
BH	Biblical Hebrew
ca.	circa
CD	Cairo Genizah copy of the *Damascus Document*
ch(s).	chapter(s)
col(s).	column(s)
cont.	continuation line
DSS	Dead Sea Scrolls
ed(s).	editor(s), edited by; or edition
esp.	especially
ET	English translation
fig.	figure
frg(s).	fragment(s)
LXX	Septuagint (the Greek version of the Old Testament/Hebrew Bible)
m.	*Mishnah*: tractate in the Mishnah
MH	Mishnaic Hebrew
MS(S)	manuscript(s)
MT	Masoretic Text (of the Hebrew Bible/Old Testament)
n.	note
NJPS	*Tanakh: The Holy Scriptures. The New JPS Translation According to the Traditional Hebrew Text*
no.	number
NRSV	New Revised Standard Version
P	Priestly source/writer of one portion of the Pentateuch
pl.	plural *or* plate
QH	Qumranic Hebrew
R.	Rabbi
repr.	reprint; reprinted
rev.	revised
RS	Ras Shamra
sg.	singular
SP	Samaritan Pentateuch
sup(pl.)	supplement
Syr.	Syriac
Tg(s).	targum(s)
trans.	translator, translated by
v(v).	verse(s)

vacat	empty space
Vg.	Vulgate
vol(s).	volume(s)

Classical

Spec.	Philo, *De specialibus legibus* II

Documents from the Judean Desert and Dead Sea Scrolls

The simplified abbreviation key provided here attempts to take into account the various systems that have emerged to refer to the Dead Sea Scrolls. One system classifies scrolls by cave number and an abbreviation of the text, so that, for example, 1QS refers to a document from Qumran Cave 1 that is also known as *Serekh ha-Yaḥad*, or "Rule of the Community." Abbreviations beginning with "4Q" indicate documents from Qumran Cave 4, and so on. Another system uses the cave number followed by a manuscript number, as in, for example, 4Q364. When multiple manuscripts of the same text are attested, they are designated with superscripted letters (a, b, c, etc.) following the document's name or siglum, as with Reworked Pentateuch[b] and Reworked Pentateuch[c]. Additional systems of naming and classification exist as well.[1] In cases where a new siglum has replaced an older one, the earlier abbreviation is included with the Latin annotation *olim* [formerly].

Abbreviation	*Official Siglum or Title*	*Name of Text*
Qumran		
1Q2	Exod	Exodus
1Q3	paleoLev	Paleo-Hebrew Leviticus scroll
1Q4	Deut[a]	Deuteronomy[a]
1Q5	Deut[b]	Deuteronomy[b]
1QIsa[a]	Isa[a]	Isaiah[a]
1QS	S (= *Serekh ha-Yaḥad*)	Rule of the Community
2Q2	Exod[a]	Exodus[a]
2Q3	Exod[b]	Exodus[b]
2Q4	Exod[c]	Exodus[c]
2Q5	paleoLev	Paleo-Hebrew Leviticus scroll
2Q6	Num[a]	Numbers[a]
2Q7	Num[b]	Numbers[b]
2Q8	Num[c]	Numbers[c]

---

1. For more detailed information, see Emanuel Tov, "Appendix F: Texts from the Judean Desert," in *The SBL Handbook of Style for Ancient Near Eastern, Biblical, and Early Christian Studies* (Peabody, MA: Hendrickson, 1999) 176–233 (see also pp. 75–77); "Provisional List of Documents from the Judean Desert," in *Encyclopedia of the Dead Sea Scrolls* (ed. Lawrence H. Schiffman and James C. VanderKam; 2 vols.; New York: Oxford University Press, 2000) 2:1013–49; and Emanuel Tov, "The Discoveries in the Judaean Desert Series: History and System of Presentation," in *The Texts from the Judaean Desert: Indices and an Introduction to the Discoveries in the Judaean Desert Series* (ed. Emanuel Tov, with contributions by Martin Abegg Jr. et al.; DJD 39; Oxford: Clarendon, 2002) 1–25.

Abbreviation	Official Siglum or Title	Name of Text
2Q9	Num^d?	Numbers^d?
2Q10	Deut^a	Deuteronomy^a
2Q11	Deut^b	Deuteronomy^b
2Q12	Deut^c	Deuteronomy^c
4Q1	Gen–Exod^a	Genesis–Exodus^a
4Q11	paleoGen–Exod^l	Paleo-Genesis-Exodus^l
4Q13	Exod^b	Exodus^b
4Q14	Exod^c	Exodus^c
4Q15	Exod^d	Exodus^d
4Q16	Exod^e	Exodus^e
4Q17	Exod^f	Exodus^f
4Q18	Exod^g	Exodus^g
4Q19	Exod^h	Exodus^h
4Q20	Exod^j	Exodus^j
4Q21	Exod^k	Exodus^k
4Q22	paleoExod^m	Paleo-Exodus^m
4Q23	Lev–Num^a	Leviticus–Numbers^a
4Q24	Lev^b	Leviticus^b
4Q25	Lev^c	Leviticus^c
4Q26	Lev^d	Leviticus^d
4Q26a	Lev^e	Leviticus^e
4Q26b	Lev^g	Leviticus^g
4Q27	Num^b	Numbers^b
4Q28–44	Deut^a–Deut^q	Deuteronomy^a–Deuteronomy^q
4Q33	Deut^f	Deuteronomy^f
4Q36	Deutⁱ	Deuteronomyⁱ
4Q38a	Deut^{k2}	Deuteronomy^{k2}
4Q45	paleoDeut^r	Paleo-Deuteronomy^r
4Q46	paleoDeut^s	Paleo-Deuteronomy^s
4Q76	XII^a	Minor Prophets^a
4Q158	RP^a (BibPar = 4QRP^a)	Reworked Pentateuch^a
4Q169	pNah	Pesher Nahum
4Q271	D^f (*olim* D^c)	Damascus Document^f
4Q364	RP^b	Reworked Pentateuch^b
4Q365	RP^c	Reworked Pentateuch^c
4Q365a	T^a?	Temple Scroll
4Q366	RP^d	Reworked Pentateuch^d
4Q367	RP^e	Reworked Pentateuch^e
4Q394–399	MMT^a–MMT^f (= *Miqṣat Maʿaśê ha-Torah*^{a–f})	MMT^a–MMT^f
4Q416	Instruction^b (= *olim* Sap. Work A^b)	Instruction^b
4Q422	ParaGen-Exod	Paraphrase of Genesis-Exodus
4Q524	T^b (= *olim* halakic text)	halakic text

Abbreviation	Official Siglum or Title	Name of Text
5Q1	Deut	Deuteronomy
6Q2	paleoLev	paleo-Leviticus
6Q3	papDeut?	Deuteronomy?
6Q20	Deut?	Deuteronomy?
8Q3	Phyl	phylactery
11Q1	paleoLev[a]	Paleo-Hebrew Leviticus[a]
11Q2	Lev[b]	Leviticus[b]
11Q3	Deut	Deuteronomy
11Q19 (11QTemple[a])[2]	T[a]	Temple Scroll[a]
11Q20	T[b]	Temple Scroll[b]
11Q21	T[c]	Temple Scroll[c]
XQ 1–4	Phyl. 1–4	Phylacteries 1–4
Masada		
Mas1a	Lev[a]	Leviticus[a]
Mas1b	Lev[b]	Leviticus[b]
Mas1c	Deut	Deuteronomy
Murabbaʿat		
Mur 1:4–5	Exod	Exodus
Mur 1:6–7	Num	Numbers
Mur 2	Deut	Deuteronomy
Naḥal Ḥever, Naḥal Ṣeʾelim		
5/6Ḥev 1a	Num[a]	Numbers[a]
XḤev/Se 1	Num[a]	Numbers[a]
XḤev/Se 2	Num[b]	Numbers[b]
XḤev/Se 3	Deut	Deuteronomy
34Se 2	Num	Numbers

Targumic and Rabbinic Sources

Exod. Rab.   *Exodus Rabbah*
Ned.   *Nedarim*
Roš Haš.   *Roš Haššanah*
Tg. Qoh.   *Targum Qoheleth*

Periodicals, Reference Works, and Series

AB   Anchor Bible

---

2. In this book, all references to 11QT without superscript refer to this manuscript.

AbrNSup	Abr-Nahrain: Supplement Series
AJP	*American Journal of Philology*
AJS Review	*Association for Jewish Studies Review*
AnOr	Analecta orientalia
AOAT	Alter Orient und Altes Testament
AOS	American Oriental Series
BDB	Brown, Francis, Samuel Rolles Driver, and Charles A. Briggs. *A Hebrew and English Lexicon of the Old Testament*. Oxford: Clarendon, 1906. Reprinted with supplement, Peabody, MA: Hendrickson, 1996
BeO	*Bibbia e oriente*
BETL	Bibliotheca ephemeridum theologicarum lovaniensium
BKAT	Biblischer Kommentar: Altes Testament
BWANT	Beiträge zur Wissenschaft vom Alten und Neuen Testament
BZAR	Beihefte zur Zeitschrift für Altorientalische und Biblische Rechtsgeschichte
BZAW	Beihefte zur Zeitschrift für die alttestamentliche Wissenschaft
CahRB	Cahiers de la Revue biblique
CBET	Contributions to Biblical Exegesis and Theology
CBQ	*Catholic Biblical Quarterly*
CC	Continental Commentaries
DJD	Discoveries in the Judaean Desert
DMOA	Documenta et Monumenta Orientis Antiqui
DSD	*Dead Sea Discoveries*
EdF	Erträge der Forschung
ErIsr	*Eretz-Israel*
ETL	*Ephemerides theologicae lovanienses*
FAT	Forschungen zum Alten Testament
GAG	Von Soden, Wolfram, with Werner R. Mayer. *Grundriss der Akkadischen Grammatik*. 3rd ed. AnOr 33. Rome: Pontifical Biblical Institute, 1995
HALOT	Koehler, Ludwig, et al. *The Hebrew and Aramaic Lexicon of the Old Testament*. Translated and ed. under supervision of M. E. J. Richardson. 5 vols. Leiden: Brill, 1994–2000
HKAT	Handkommentar zum Alten Testament
HS	*Hebrew Studies*
HSM	Harvard Semitic Monographs
HSS	Harvard Semitic Studies
HTR	*Harvard Theological Review*
HUCA	*Hebrew Union College Annual*
ICC	International Critical Commentary
JAOS	*Journal of the American Oriental Society*
JBL	*Journal of Biblical Literature*
JHS	*Journal of Hebrew Scriptures*, http://www.jhsonline.org
JJS	*Journal of Jewish Studies*
JNSL	*Journal of Northwest Semitic Languages*
JSHJ	*Journal for the Study of the Historical Jesus*
JSHRZ	Jüdische Schriften aus hellenistisch-römischer Zeit

JSJ	*Journal for the Study of Judaism in the Persian, Hellenistic, and Roman Periods*
JSJSup	Journal for the Study of Judaism in the Persian, Hellenistic, and Roman Periods: Supplement Series
JSOTSup	Journal for the Study of the Old Testament Supplement Series
KHC	Kurzer Hand-Commentar zum Alten Testament
MdB	Le Monde de la Bible
NCB	New Century Bible
NEchtB	Neue Echter Bibel
OBO	Orbis biblicus et orientalis
OLA	Orientalia lovaniensia analecta
OtSt	Oudtestamentische Studiën
RBL	*Review of Biblical Literature,* http://www.bookreviews.org
RevQ	*Revue de Qumran*
SAOC	Studies in Ancient Oriental Civilization
SBAB	Stuttgarter biblische Aufsatzbände
SBLMasS	Society of Biblical Literature Masoretic Studies
SBLRBS	Society of Biblical Literature Resources for Biblical Study
SBLSCS	Society of Biblical Literature Septuagint and Cognate Studies
SBLWAW	Society of Biblical Literature Writings from the Ancient World
ScrHier	Scripta hierosolymitana
STDJ	Studies on the Texts of the Desert of Judah
SubBi	Subsidia Biblica
TDOT	Botterweck, G. Johannes, Heinz-Josef Fabry, and Helmer Ringgren, eds. *Theological Dictionary of the Old Testament.* Translated by J. T. Willis, G. W. Bromiley, and D. E. Green. 15 vols. Grand Rapids, MI: Eerdmans, 1974–2006
TLZ	*Theologische Literaturzeitung*
TZ	*Theologische Zeitschrift*
UF	*Ugarit-Forschungen*
VT	*Vetus Testamentum*
VTSup	Supplements to Vetus Testamentum
WMANT	Wissenschaftliche Monographien zum Alten und Neuen Testament
WZKM	*Wiener Zeitschrift für die Kunde des Morgenlandes*
ZABR	*Zeitschrift für Altorientalische und Biblische Rechtsgeschichte*
ZAH	*Zeitschrift für Althebräistik*
ZAW	*Zeitschrift für die alttestamentliche Wissenschaft*
ZDMGSup	Zeitschrift der deutschen morgenlandischen Gesellschaft: Supplementbände

PART I

Revelation Regained:
The Hermeneutics of כי *and* אם
in the Temple Scroll

I. Previous Attempts to Provide a Solution:
The Problem of Method

The frequent replacement of conditional כי, "if," with its semantic equivalent, אם, in the Temple Scroll has been well documented. The replacement appears in some cases where the redactor incorporated biblical laws that employ כי to mark the "if" clause, or protasis. A clear example is the Temple Scroll's reuse of Deuteronomy's law against apostasy. Figure I.I shows the substitution of אם for כי, which is here accompanied by other signs of linguistic updating that characterize the reception of the biblical text in the Second Temple period (such as the plene spelling of the second-person suffix).[1]

| Deut 13:2a | כִּי יקום בקרבך נביא או חלם חלום | *If* a prophet or oneiro-mancer arises among you |
| 11QT 54:8 | אִם יקום בקרבכה נביא או חולם חלום | *If* a prophet or oneiro-mancer arises among you |

FIGURE I.I. The Replacement in the Temple Scroll

The two protases in the above example are equivalent in meaning; at issue is the rationale for the lexical substitution. This problem has not yet received a satisfactory explanation. In the Temple Scroll's *editio princeps*, Yigael Yadin noted the change and attributed it to the redactor's attempts to write biblically: the substitution was made to imitate the casuistic style of Leviticus.[2] Gershon Brin promptly rejected this explanation, since no

---

1. Two works, in particular, have helped place the study of the orthography, phonology, morphology, and syntax of Qumran Hebrew on a solid foundation: Eduard Y. Kutscher, *The Language and Linguistic Background of the Isaiah Scroll (1QIsaᵃ)* (ed. Elisha Qimron; STDJ 6A; 2nd ed.; Leiden: Brill, 1979; Hebrew original, 1959); and Elisha Qimron, *The Hebrew of the Dead Sea Scrolls* (HSS 29; Atlanta: Scholars Press, 1986).

2. Yigael Yadin, מגילת המקדש (4 vols., Jerusalem: Israel Exploration Society, 1977) 2:174. The English translation expands the Hebrew original; see idem, *The Temple Scroll* (3 vols.; Jerusalem: Israel Exploration Society, 1977–83) 2:247. All subsequent citations are to the English edition. Unless otherwise noted, all references to the Temple Scroll in this book refer to manuscript 11Q19 = 11QTemple Scrollᵃ. For critical editions of the A copy, see Yadin, *Temple Scroll*; Lawrence H. Schiffman [with James H. Charlesworth et al.], *The Dead Sea Scrolls: Hebrew, Aramaic, and Greek Texts with English Translations*, vol. 7: *Temple Scroll and Related Documents* (Princeton Theological Seminary Dead Sea Scrolls Project; Tübingen: Mohr Siebeck / Louisville: Westminster John Knox, 2011) 12–173; and Elisha Qimron,

biblical laws (including those of Leviticus) begin with the formula (+ אם
יקטל).[3] Brin sought an alternative explanation in terms of historical linguistics. By the time the Temple Scroll was redacted, כי had fallen out of
use, he argued, so the redactor replaced it with אם, which had emerged as
the standard conditional in Second Temple Hebrew. More recently, Takamitsu Muraoka has introduced an important new factor into this discussion, proposing that the replacement responds to the intrinsic ambiguity
of the particle כי itself. Attempting to gain "the maximum efficiency of
communication," Qumran Hebrew will occasionally replace כי, a conjunction that has a wide range of unrelated meanings, with אם, which functions
solely as a conditional.[4] Muraoka correctly points out, however, that the
story is more complicated, because there was a continuing "toleration" of
כי in the DSS despite its ambiguity.[5] Precisely this recognition points to a
difficulty in the explanatory model.

Muraoka attempts to identify linguistic "isoglosses"—features of syntax, orthography, and morphology that distinguish one dialect from another—in order to learn more about the distinctive "nature of Qumran
Hebrew."[6] He carefully notes that some of these features, rather than indi-
cating a genuine linguistic development, may represent literary phenomena specific to a particular copyist, author, or genre.[7] The astute method
that he employs (building on the prior work of Kutscher and Bendavid) of
searching for QH's divergences from BH as reflected in the transmission
and reuse of the biblical text, thus entails an inherent ambiguity about
whether any given isogloss represents a matter of "language" or a matter
of "text." Although Muraoka allows for the latter possibility elsewhere in
his article,[8] it does not enter into his analysis of the replacement. There,
the analytical model remains one-sidedly a model of historical linguistics.

מגילות מדבר יהודה: החיבורים העבריים, *The Dead Sea Scrolls: The Hebrew Writings*, vol. I (3 vols.;
Between Bible and Mishnah; Jerusalem: Yad Ben-Zvi, 2010) 137–207 [Hebrew; English in-
troduction], superseding Qimron's 1996 edition; see bibliography.

3. Gershon Brin, "The Bible as Reflected in the Temple Scroll," *Shnaton: Annual for
Biblical and Ancient Near Eastern Studies* 4 (ed. Moshe Weinfeld; Jerusalem: Israel Bible
Society, 1980) 182–224 (at pp. 214–17) (Hebrew; English abstract). Brin's challenge responds
to Yadin's Hebrew original; in the later English edition cited above, Yadin provides a brief
response to the challenge (*Temple Scroll*, 2:247).

4. Takamitsu Muraoka, "An Approach to the Morphosyntax and Syntax of Qumran
Hebrew," in *Diggers at the Well: Proceedings of a Third International Symposium on the Hebrew of the Dead Sea Scrolls and Ben Sira* (ed. Takamitsu Muraoka and John F. Elwolde; STDJ
36; Leiden: Brill, 2000) 192–214 (at p. 212).

5. Ibid., 213.

6. Ibid., 193.

7. Ibid., 193, 214.

8. Muraoka considers it likely, for example, that the mixed use of the *waw*-conversive
alongside non-converted forms in a single manuscript indicates a single scribe's attempt to
negotiate between the differing syntactical structures of Biblical and Mishnaic Hebrew. The

Yet it is precisely in this last of his isoglosses where the "textual" nature of the phenomenon is salient. The list of examples that Muraoka himself provides demonstrates that the replacement of כי with אם is text-specific. It appears ten times in the Temple Scroll[9] and once in 4Q158.[10] It appears only in these two manuscripts. It does not occur in the rest of the Reworked Pentateuch (4Q364–367).[11] Nor does it appear in any of the biblical manuscripts from Qumran, as a check of all the published fragments containing material from Exodus through Deuteronomy confirms.[12]

---

phenomenon does not, therefore, represent a distinctive characteristic of Qumran Hebrew (ibid., 212).

9. The replacement occurs in 11QTemple 43:13; 52:9; 53:12; 54:8, 19; 55:2, 13, 15; 58:15; 61:7. Nine of the ten cases are noted by Brin ("Bible in Temple Scroll," 215) and by Yohanan Thorion ("Die Sprache der Tempelrolle und die Chronikbücher," *RevQ* 11 [1982–84] 423–26 [at p. 423]). Muraoka lists six of them ("Morphosyntax," 213).

10. Thorion, "Sprache der Tempelrolle," 423; and Muraoka, "Morphosyntax," 213.

11. None of the other manuscripts of the Temple Scroll (11Q20 = 11QTemple Scroll[b]; 11Q21 = 11QTemple Scroll[c]; 4Q524 = T[b] [halakic text]; and 4Q365a) provides any relevant evidence. In no case is a portion of the text preserved that, in the A copy, contains an instance of the replacement or of the retention of casuistic כי. It is thus impossible to determine whether or not the change occurred in the other copies.

For 11Q20 and 11Q21, see Florentino García Martínez, Eibert J. C. Tigchelaar, and Adam S. van der Woude, eds., *Qumran Cave 11 (11Q2–18, 11Q20–31)* (DJD 23; Oxford: Clarendon, 1998) 357–414; Charlesworth et al., *Temple Scroll and Related Documents*, 182–225, 230–33; and Qimron, מגילות מדבר יהודה, *Dead Sea Scrolls*, 1:137–207.

Several cases of changes or retentions are reconstructed in the critical edition of 4Q524, but these reconstructions are dependent on 11QTemple Scroll[a] and, therefore, do not constitute an independent witness. See Émile Puech, "Fragments du plus ancien exemplaire du Rouleau du Temple (4Q524)," in *Legal Texts and Legal Issues: Proceedings of the Second Meeting of the International Organization for Qumran Studies* (ed. Moshe J. Bernstein, Florentino García Martínez, and John Kampen; STDJ 23; Leiden: Brill, 1997) 19–52 [the preliminary publication]; and idem, *Textes Hébreux (4Q521–528, 4Q576–579): Qumran Cave 4.XVIII* (DJD 25; Oxford: Clarendon, 1998) 85–114. See also Charlesworth et al., *Temple Scroll and Related Documents*, 254–65; and Qimron, מגילות מדבר יהודה, *Dead Sea Scrolls*, 1:137–207.

For 4Q365a, see Harold Attridge et al., eds., *Qumran Cave 4.VIII: Parabiblical Texts, Part 1* (DJD 13; Oxford: Clarendon, 1994) 255–318; Charlesworth et al., *Temple Scroll and Related Documents*, 254–65; and Qimron, מגילות מדבר יהודה, *Dead Sea Scrolls*, 1:137–207.

12. In order to check any biblical manuscripts that may contain casuistic law, we have examined all of the published fragments of Exodus, Leviticus, Numbers, and Deuteronomy. For 1QExod, 1QpaleoLev, 1QDeut[a], 1QDeut[b] (= 1Q2–5), see Dominique Barthélemy and Józef T. Milik, eds., *Qumran Cave 1* (DJD 1; Oxford: Clarendon, 1955). For MurExod, MurNum, MurDeut (= Mur 1:4–5, Mur 1:6–7, Mur 2), see Pierre Benoit, Józef T. Milik, and Roland de Vaux, eds., *Les grottes de Murabba'ât* (DJD 2; Oxford: Clarendon, 1961). For 2QExod[a]–Exod[c], 2QpaleoLev, 2QNum[a]–Num[d?], 2QDeut[a]–Deut[c], 5QDeut, 6QpaleoLev, 6QpapDeut?, 6QDeut?, 8QPhyl (= 2Q2–12, 5Q1, 6Q2–3, 20, 8Q3), see M. Baillet, Józef T. Milik, and Roland de Vaux, eds., *Les "petites grottes" de Qumran* (DJD 3; Oxford: Clarendon, 1962). For 4QpaleoGen–Exod[l], 4QpaleoExod[m], 4QpaleoDeut[r]–paleoDeut[s] (= 4Q11, 22, 45–46), see Patrick Skehan, Eugene Ulrich, and Judith Sanderson, eds., *Qumran Cave 4.IV: Paleo-Hebrew and Greek Biblical Manuscripts* (DJD 9; Oxford: Clarendon, 1992). For 4QGen–Exod[a], 4QExod[b]–Exod[k], 4QLev–Num[a], 4QLev[b]–Lev[g], 4QNum[b] (= 4Q1, 13–21, 23–27), see Eugene Ulrich et al., eds., *Qumran Cave 4.VII: Genesis to Numbers* (DJD 12; Oxford: Clarendon, 1994). For ParaGen–Exod (= 4Q422), see Harold Attridge et al., eds.,

Moreover, even in the two manuscripts where the replacement does occur, כי is more frequently retained than replaced. In 4Q158 frgs. 10–12, the MT's כי is replaced with אם in line 4 but preserved in lines 6 and 9.[13] The Temple Scroll retains כי 14 times, while replacing it 10 times.[14] The change is also meaning-specific. It only occurs when כי functions as a conditional to mark the protasis of a casuistic law; never, for example, when the particle begins a motive clause, where it would mean "because."

The specificity of the replacement thus calls into question a strictly linguistic approach. Historical linguistics can outline the development whereby אם would be preferred over כי, either because אם was the vernacular (Brin) or because its meaning was unambiguous (Muraoka). But it cannot account for the distribution of the replacement, which is confined almost entirely to the Temple Scroll. Nor can it account for the Temple Scroll's simultaneous retention of כי, which runs contrary to expectation. The phenomenon of the replacement in the Temple Scroll thus challenges the explanatory power of historical linguistics and mandates a new conceptual model.

II. An Alternative Approach: Rethinking the Problem of כי

An approach that integrates historical linguistics with literary history and hermeneutics is necessary. Brin and Muraoka are correct to point out that the conjunction כי had to have been a problem for any Second

---

Qumran Cave 4.VIII: Parabiblical Texts, Part 1 (DJD 13; Oxford: Clarendon, 1994). For 4QDeut^a–Deut^q (= 4Q28–44), see Eugene Ulrich et al., eds., *Qumran Cave 4.IX: Deuteronomy, Joshua, Judges, Kings* (DJD 14; Oxford: Clarendon, 1995). For 11QpaleoLev^a (= 11Q1), see David N. Freedman and K. A. Mathews, *The Paleo-Hebrew Leviticus Scroll (11QpaleoLev)* (Philadelphia: ASOR, 1985). For 11QLev^b and 11QDeut (= 11Q2–3), see Martínez, Tigchelaar, and van der Woude, eds., *Qumran Cave 11, 5/6HevNum^a, XHev/SeNum^a–Num^b, XHev/SeDeut, 34SeNum* (= 5/6Hev1a, XHev/Se 1–2, XHev/Se 3, 34Se 2), see James Charlesworth et al., eds., *Miscellaneous Texts from the Judaean Desert* (DJD 38; Oxford: Clarendon, 2000). For XQ Phyl 1–4 (= XQ 1–4), see Yigael Yadin, *Tefillin from Qumran* (Jerusalem: Israel Exploration Society and the Shrine of the Book, 1969). For MasLev^a–Lev^b, MasDeut (Mas1a–Mas1b, Mas1c), see Shemaryahu Talmon and Yigael Yadin, eds., *Masada VI: Yigael Yadin Excavations 1963–1965 Final Reports* (Jerusalem: Israel Exploration Society and Hebrew University of Jerusalem, 1999).

13. See John M. Allegro, ed., *Qumran Cave 4.1 (4Q158–4Q186)* (DJD 5; Oxford: Clarendon, 1968) 5. The two instances where MT כי is retained are cited by Muraoka as examples of the toleration of the "archaic use" ("Morphosyntax," 213, where the second case of retention, by typo, is cited as line 8).

14. 11QTemple retains the original כי from its Deuteronomic source text in 56:12; 60:12, 16; 61:12; 62:5; 63:10; 64:2, 6, 9; 65:2, 5, 6, 7; 66:8. The Priestly *casus pendens* form (איש כי) is reproduced in 11QTemple 45:7; 53:14, 16.

Temple reader. With 4,475 attestations distributed across every genre and book of the Bible, it was second only to paratactic -וְ as the most frequent clause connector in Biblical Hebrew.[15] Yet, like *k*, its cognate in Ugaritic,[16] Hebrew כִּי had a wide range of unrelated meanings that were not always easily distinguished in particular cases.[17] Its diverse uses included introducing (1) a conditional clause ("if"); (2) a relative clause ("that"); (3) a temporal clause ("when");[18] (4) an explanatory clause ("because"); or (5) an asseveration ("truly," "indeed").[19] The particle's complexity was already

---

15. Noted by Anneli Aejmelaeus, "The Function and Interpretation of כִּי in Biblical Hebrew," *JBL* 105 (1986) 193–209; repr. in *On the Trail of Septuagint Translators: Collected Essays* (Kampen: Kok Pharos, 1993) 166–85 (at p. 166). For the frequency, see Abraham Even-Shoshan, ed., *A New Concordance of the Old Testament* (2nd ed.; Jerusalem: Kiryat Sefer, 1997) 529–33.

16. Josef Tropper, *Ugaritische Grammatik* (AOAT 273; Münster: Ugarit-Verlag, 2000) 801–2 (§83.24b), 909 (§97.91).

17. In his analysis of כִּי in the Pentateuch and the Psalms, Barry L. Bandstra demonstrates the connection between the semantic value of כִּי and its position in the sentence. For example, a clause with conditional כִּי always precedes the main clause, whereas a clause in which כִּי is causative follows the main clause. See idem, *The Syntax of Particle* כִּי *in Hebrew and Ugaritic* (Ph.D. diss., Yale University, 1982) 408. Bandstra argues that כִּי is a "clause relator particle" (pp. 12–13). With this valuable insight, he identifies syntax and semantics, controlled by comparative Semitics, as the proper basis for understanding the particle; he thus properly breaks free of models that reduce the particle to its alleged etymological origins in deixis. See further n. 27 below.

18. Surprisingly, the new *Dictionary of Classical Hebrew* fails to distinguish between the conditional ("if") and temporal ("when") functions of כִּי ([8 vols.; ed. D. J. A. Clines; Sheffield: Sheffield Academic Press, 1993–2011] 4:386–87). The technical use of כִּי to introduce a legal protasis is also omitted. Thus, despite the comprehensive inclusion of data from Biblical, Inscriptional, and Qumran Hebrew, the *Dictionary* overlooks essential semantic distinctions when it comes to analyzing this material. For an incisive assessment raising other issues, see Takamitsu Muraoka, "A New Dictionary of Classical Hebrew," in *Studies in Ancient Hebrew Semantics* (ed. T. Muraoka; AbrNSup 4; Louvain: Peeters, 1995) 87–101. On the problem of distinguishing the temporal and conditional use of the conjunction, see also n. 38 below.

19. James Muilenburg attempts to derive the full range of functions of the conjunction from the single rubric of "emphasis"; see idem, "The Linguistic and Rhetorical Uses of the Particle כִּי in the Old Testament," *HUCA* 32 (1961) 135–60; repr. in *Hearing and Speaking the Word* (ed. T. F. Best; Chico, CA: Scholars Press, 1984) 208–33. In elevating emphasis to a universal, portmanteau category, Muilenburg pays scant attention to other uses of the conjunction (for example, as the protasis marker of casuistic law). With their clear literary history, these uses challenge the model's romantic assumptions about the primitive origins of language in deixis and onomatopoeia. On different grounds, Muilenburg has received important challenges from Walter T. Claassen, "Speaker-Oriented Functions of *Kî* in Biblical Hebrew," *JNSL* 11 (1983) 29–46; and Takamitsu Muraoka, *Emphatic Words and Structures in Biblical Hebrew* (Jerusalem: Magnes / Leiden: Brill, 1985) 158–64. Independent studies of the particle include Anton Schoors, "The Particle כִּי," in *Remembering All the Way . . .* (ed. Bertil Albrektson et al.; OtSt 21; Leiden: Brill, 1981) 240–76; Bandstra, *Syntax of Particle* כִּי; Yochanon [Yohanan] Thorion, *Studien zur klassischen hebräischen Syntax* (Marburger Studien zur Afrika- und Asienkunde B/6; Berlin: Reimer, 1984) 1–37; Aejmelaeus, "Function and Interpretation," 166–85; and Carl M. Follingstad, *Deictic Viewpoint in Biblical Hebrew*

identified in antiquity as a problem of legal hermeneutics.[20]

The polyvalence of the conjunction inevitably required a move toward lexical simplification in the course of the reception, translation, and exegesis of the biblical text.[21] The diachronic development of the spoken language would equally have mandated such a change. The problem at issue in the replacement, however, is not כי in general but its specific use as a conditional marker in a legal protasis. This function required special attention because it was, almost certainly, literary and classical rather than vernacular. In the entire corpus of inscriptional and epigraphic Hebrew, there is not a single attestation of conditional כי. Rather, "אם is the marker of the protasis of a conditional sentence in epigraphic Hebrew."[22] In contrast, כי was employed to mark a relative clause ("that"), an explanatory clause ("because" or "seeing that"), or an oath formula.[23]

The hypothesis that the protasis-marking function of כי was primarily a literary and scribal use receives additional confirmation from the corpus of biblical law. The casuistic laws of the Covenant Code, in the use of the conditional form as well as in terminology and content, closely reflect the legacy of the great cuneiform legal collections. In particular, the specific role assigned to כי corresponds precisely to the formal protasis marker used in cuneiform law: Sumerian *tukumbi*, Akkadian *šumma*, and Hittite *takku*.[24] Indeed, this casuistic form was not restricted to law. It provided

---

Text: A Syntagmatic and Paradigmatic Analysis of the Particle כי (Dallas: SIL, 2001). For further discussion of key articles cited here, see also nn. 21, 27, 38, and 69 below.

20. Talmudic hermeneutics delineated five distinct meanings for the particle. Apart from meaning "that" (following verbs of speech or vision, where it serves as a relative conjunction), the Amora Resh Laqish maintained: כי משמש בארבע לשונות: אי, דהא, אלא, דילמא, "*kî* serves for four [additional] idioms: 'if,' 'perhaps,' 'but,' 'for'" (*b. Roš Haš.* 3a [translation mine]; also noted by Avigdor Shinan, *Midrash Shemot Rabbah, Chapters I–XIV: A Critical Edition Based on a Jerusalem Manuscript with Variants, Commentary, and Introduction* [Jerusalem: Dvir, 1984] 207 [Hebrew]). A similar ancient recognition of the particle's polysemy is made explicit in *Exodus Rabbah*'s discussion of its temporal versus conditional force in Exod 7:9a (see n. 38 below).

21. Contra Schoors, for whom "[t]he diminution of its use in later Hebrew, when compared to its high frequency in the Bible, is rather strange" ("Particle כי," 240). The combination of the frequency and the multiplicity of meanings provides, to the contrary, the best explanation for its "diminution."

22. See Sandra L. Gogel, *A Grammar of Epigraphic Hebrew* (SBLRBS 23; Atlanta: Scholars Press, 1998) 224. The syntax of conditional sentences and the relevant particles is overlooked by Andreas Schüle, *Die Syntax der althebräischen Inschriften: Ein Beitrag zur historischen Grammatik des Hebräischen* (AOAT 270; Münster: Ugarit-Verlag, 2000).

23. See Gogel, *Epigraphic Hebrew*, 226–29.

24. Roderick A. F. Mackenzie shows how the Hebrew conditional corresponds to Sumerian *tukumbi* and Akkadian *šumma*, in "The Formal Aspect of Ancient Near Eastern Law," in *The Seed of Wisdom: Essays in Honor of T. J. Meek* (ed. W. S. McCullough; Toronto: University of Toronto Press, 1964) 31–44. See further Stanislav Segert, "Form and Function of An-

a literary matrix for the compilation of the scientific knowledge of the ancient Near East, where it was employed in collections of omens, incantations, dreams, medical texts, and laws.[25] The technical use of *k* in the Ugaritic Hippiatric corpus to mark the protasis of a "case" in veterinary medicine equally reflects this casuistic genre.[26] Previous studies that focus on the syntax of כִּי have recognized the analogy with Ugaritic *k* in general terms but have not noted its restricted technical use in the Hippiatric corpus. With regard to Akkadian, the tendency is to bring into the discussion only explicitly homologous forms such as *kī*, *kīma*, and *kīam*. As a result, studies of this sort have failed to recognize the far more relevant analogy to Akkadian *šumma* as the conjunction that formally marks the protasis of a casuistic sentence. Once this analogy is seen, it becomes clear that the semantics of כִּי as protasis marker are tied to a specific literary genre.[27]

The original technical and literary use of conditional כִּי, combined with the particle's intrinsic polyvalence, militated against its retention in vernacular speech or writing in the Second Temple period. Indeed its fos-

---

cient Israelite, Greek and Roman Legal Sentences," in *Orient and Occident: Essays Presented to Cyrus H. Gordon on the Occasion of His Sixty-Fifth Birthday* (ed. Harry A. Hoffner; AOAT 22; Kevelaer: Butzon & Bercker / Neukirchen-Vluyn: Neukirchener Verlag, 1973) 151–59.

25. See Benno Landsberger, "Die Eigenbegrifflichkeit der babylonischen Welt," *Islamica* 2 (1926) 355–72 (at pp. 370–71); ET, *The Conceptual Autonomy of the Babylonian World* (trans. Thorkild Jacobsen, Benjamin R. Foster, and Heinrich von Siebenthal; Monographs of the Ancient Near East 1/4; Malibu, CA: Undena, 1976) 3–15 (at pp. 14–15); F. R. Kraus, "Ein zentrales Problem des altmesopotamischen Rechts: Was ist der Codex Hammurabi," *Genava* 8 (1960) 283–96 (at pp. 288, 293); and especially Jean Bottéro, *Mesopotamia: Writing, Reasoning, and the Gods* (Chicago: University of Chicago Press, 1992) 113–24, 169–77.

26. The correspondence of Ugaritic *k* to Akkadian *šumma* escapes Tropper, *Ugaritische Grammatik*, 800 (§83.24). Previously recognizing the equivalence are Cyrus H. Gordon, "Review of E. Ebeling, *Bruchstücke einer mittelassyrischen Vorschriftensammlung für die Akklimatisierung und Trainierung von Wagenpferden*," *Orientalia* 22 (1953) 231–32; and T. L. Fenton, "The Claremont 'Mrzḥ' Tablet, Its Text and Meaning," *UF* 9 (1977) 71–75 (at pp. 73–74). It is also noted in the two excellent editions of the Hippiatric corpus that, by chance, were prepared independently of each other; see Chaim Cohen and Daniel Sivan, *The Ugaritic Hippiatric Texts: A Critical Edition* (AOS 9; New Haven, CT: American Oriental Society, 1983); and Dennis Pardee, *Les Textes Hippiatriques: Ras Shamra–Ougarit II* (Paris: Editions Recherche sur les Civilisations, 1985). Both editions provide valuable discussions of the syntax of *k*. For the latest edition, see Chaim Cohen, "The Ugaritic Hippiatric Texts: Revised Composite Text, Translation, and Commentary," *UF* 28 (1996) 105–53. On *k* as consistently marking the protasis, see earlier A. M. Honeyman, "Varia Punica," *American Journal of Philology* 68 (1947) 77–82 (at p. 81).

27. An important advance in this regard is made by Bandstra, who for the first time brings into consideration the Ugaritic Hippiatric material. However, he does not fully realize the promise of this insight: like his predecessor, Schoors, he overlooks the connection with Akkadian *šumma*. (See Bandstra, *Syntax of Particle* כִּי, 361–62, 402–5; Schoors, "Particle כִּי," 242.) The use of *k* in the Ugaritic Hippiatric corpus reflects *šumma* as employed in Akkadian Hippiatric texts. See Cohen and Sivan, *Ugaritic Hippiatric Texts*, 1–3, 11; and Pardee, *Textes Hippiatriques*, 41, 75.

silization and disappearance are evident both biblically and nonbiblically. It is already apparent in Qoheleth's reuse of Deuteronomy's law of vows. The ambiguous conditional of the source is defined and delimited as a temporal marker:

כִּי תִדֹּר נֶדֶר לַיהוה אֱלֹהֶיךָ לֹא תְאַחֵר לְשַׁלְּמוֹ

If you make a vow to Yahweh your God, do not delay in fulfilling it. (Deut 23:22)

כַּאֲשֶׁר תִּדֹּר נֶדֶר לֵאלֹהִים אַל תְּאַחֵר לְשַׁלְּמוֹ

When you make a vow to God, do not delay in fulfilling it. (Qoh 5:3)

The Chronicler used כי almost exclusively in its causal function and only very rarely to introduce a conditional or temporal clause.[28] The same holds true for Ben Sira, where כי occurs 109 times but only 4 times as a conditional.[29] In 2 of these cases, כי is understood as causal by one of the versions, highlighting all the more the obsolescence of its conditional meaning.[30] The normal conditional marker in Ben Sira is אם.[31]

Examination of several Qumran texts confirms that, by late Second Temple times, אם had become the standard conditional.[32] In the critical

---

28. See Arno Kropat, *Die Syntax des Autors der Chronik* (BZAW 16; Gießen: Alfred Töpelmann, 1909) 68–69.

29. See Wido T. van Peursen, "Conditional Sentences with אם in the Protasis in Qumran Hebrew," in *Diggers at the Well: Proceedings of a Third International Symposium on the Hebrew of the Dead Sea Scrolls and Ben Sira* (ed. Takamitsu Muraoka and John F. Elwolde; STDJ 36; Leiden: Brill, 2000) 214–31 (at p. 231). In contrast, Menachem Zevi Kaddari identifies only one occurrence of conditional כי; see idem, "The Syntax of כי in the Language of Ben Sira," in *The Hebrew of the Dead Sea Scrolls and Ben Sira* (ed. Takamitsu Muraoka and John F. Elwolde; STDJ 26; Leiden: Brill, 1997) 87–91. Kaddari demonstrates that, while all of the uses of כי in Ben Sira are also attested in Biblical Hebrew, the full range of classical uses is not preserved in Ben Sira. His list of the functions of כי in Biblical Hebrew, however, overlooks its role in biblical casuistic law.

30. In Sir 16:2b, MS A reads אם, while MS B has כי. The variants most likely simply represent two alternative ways of expressing the conditional. The Syriac, however, does not recognize the conditional use of כי and translates the phrase as causal (see van Peursen, "Conditional Sentences," 231). A similar translation of conditional כי into its more recognizable, causal meaning appears in the LXX of Sir 16:22; see Steven E. Fassberg, "On the Syntax of Dependent Clauses in Ben Sira," in *The Hebrew of the Dead Sea Scrolls and Ben Sira* (ed. Takamitsu Muraoka and John F. Elwolde; STDJ 26; Leiden: Brill, 1997) 56–71 (at p. 60 n. 19). Following the LXX reading of Sir 16:22, see Patrick Skehan and Alexander A. DiLella, *The Wisdom of Ben Sira* (AB 39; New York: Doubleday, 1987) 269. The Hebrew could also, in fact, be understood as emphatic: *wahrlich*; see Georg Sauer, *Unterweisungen in lehrhafter Form: Jesus Sirach (Ben Sira)* (JSHRZ 3; Gütersloh: Mohn, 1981) 545.

31. See Fassberg, "Syntax," 58–60.

32. This expansion of the range of functions of אם in Qumran Hebrew so that it assumes specific conditional functions that were reserved for כי in the classical language is

edition of *Miqṣat Maʿaśe ha-Torah* (4QMMT), conditional כי does not occur in the extant manuscript; its reconstruction by the editors in a single instance is open to question.[33] In the *Damascus Document* (CD), אם is used 33 times to mark the conditional; כי never serves this purpose.[34] And in *Serekh ha-Yaḥad* (1QS), conditional כי occurs only once, versus 18 times for conditional אם.[35] To summarize: of the 85 total occurrences of כי in 4QMMT, CD, and 1QS, only 1 is clearly conditional.[36]

The climax of this process is the disappearance of conditional כי in Rabbinic Hebrew.[37] As in the Dead Sea Scrolls, אם emerges as the standard conditional.[38] The nonretention of כי as the marker of a legal case thus represents one of the major distinctions between Classical and Rabbinic

---

overlooked by John F. Elwolde, "Non-Biblical Supplements to Classical Hebrew ʾIM," *VT* 40 (1990) 221–23. For example, Biblical Hebrew restricted אם to marking the subconditions of a casuistic law (see §VI below), whereas in Qumran Hebrew it routinely marks the main clause (as in 11QTemple, 1QS, and 4Q158).

33. B 27 in the composite text (reconstructed based on 4Q394–4Q399); see Elisha Qimron and John Strugnell, *Qumran Cave 4.V: Miqṣat Maʿaśe ha-Torah* (DJD 10; Oxford: Clarendon, 1994) 48. As the editors point out, 4QMMT here presents a paraphrase of the Priestly law prohibiting nonsacrificial slaughter in or near the camp (p. 156). In the MT, this law begins with a common Priestly *casus pendens*, איש איש מבית ישראל אשר, "As for any Israelite man who . . ." (Lev 17:4). Since the extant text of 4QMMT leaves insufficient space for this phrase, the editors logically propose a shorter phrase that is found elsewhere in Leviticus: איש כי, "a man who" (Lev 15:16; 19:20; 22:14, 21). However, the specific literary and legal context of the source chapter precludes this reconstruction: the laws of sacrifice in Leviticus 17 never employ כי as a protasis marker. Instead, it is restricted to introducing motive clauses (Lev 17:11, 14); instead, it is אשר that is consistently employed for the protasis (17:3, 8, 10, 13, 15). Therefore, an alternative reconstruction, one appropriate both to the space available in the manuscript and to the use of language in the specific source text would be (ו)אשר איש, which is very well attested (Lev 15:5; 20:10–21).

34. Joseph M. Baumgarten, *Qumran Cave 4.XIII: The Damascus Document (4Q266–273)* (DJD 18; Oxford: Clarendon, 1996).

35. See James H. Charlesworth et al., eds., *The Dead Sea Scrolls: Hebrew, Aramaic, and Greek Texts with English Translations,* vol. 1: *Rule of the Community and Related Documents,* (Princeton Theological Seminary Dead Sea Scrolls Project; Tübingen: Mohr Siebeck / Louisville: Westminster John Knox, 1994) 1–51. The one occurrence of the conditional, in the form כי איש (6:11), confirms the writer's distance from Biblical Hebrew, which requires [כי + verb in the imperfect], not [כי + subject noun].

36. For tables analyzing the full distribution and use of כי and אם in these texts, please see appendix 1.

37. See Miguel Pérez-Fernández, *An Introductory Grammar of Rabbinic Hebrew* (trans. John F. Elwolde; Leiden: Brill, 1999) 51, 192, 205, 213, 222, 240.

38. The complete loss of a conditional function for כי is evident in the relatively late *Exodus Rabbah*, where precisely the use of כי, rather than אם, in a biblical lemma is construed as proof that the protasis in question must surely represent a temporal—rather than a conditional—clause:

"אם ידבר אליכם פרעה" אין כתיב כאן, אלא: "כי ידבר אליכם [פרעה]"—עתיד הוא לומר לכם כן.

Hebrew.[39] The use or nonuse of conditional כי is as sure an isogloss be-tween the two layers of the language as is the shift from the classical aspect system of the verb to the later "tense" system.[40] The following chart sum-marizes this development away from conditional כי:

Conditional Marker	Biblical	Epi-graphic	Dead Sea Scrolls		Rabbinic
			Biblical[41]	Nonbiblical	
כי	+	—	+	—	—

FIGURE 1.2. The Loss of כי as Protasis Marker

Second Temple literature overwhelmingly rejected כי and found other ways of writing conditional legal sentences. This fact makes the Temple

---

Written here is not "*If* Pharoah should speak to you" but, rather, "*When* Pharoah speaks to you" [Exod 7:9a]: [which means,] *He is destined* to speak to you in this manner. (*Exod. Rab.* 9:1, lines 12–13)

The classical conditional use of the conjunction—here the more likely usage—has simply been lost in this case as a live option. Ironically, although unaware of this rabbinic precedent, Schoors uses the same biblical lemma to identify the same semantic difficulty: the problem of distinguishing between conditional and temporal uses of the conjunction ("Particle כי," 269). The Hebrew citation from the midrash follows the critical edition: Shinan, *Midrash Shemot Rabbah*, 207; our emphasis, punctuation, and translation.

39. On the conditional as an isogloss, see Abba Bendavid, *Biblical Hebrew and Mish-naic Hebrew* (2 vols.; Tel Aviv: Dvir, 1967–71) 2:614 (§שׁטשׁ); similarly, 1:261 (Hebrew); and Pérez-Fernández, *Grammar*, 214. The climax of this process is the complete absence of כי as conditional from the lexicon of Modern Hebrew. Strikingly, there is no reference whatsoever to the classical conditional in Tali Bar, "Expression of Temporality, Modality, and Perfectivity in Contemporary Hebrew Conditionals as Compared with Non-Conditionals," *WZKM* 91 (2001) 49–81.

40. The diachronic importance of the loss of conditional כי has not always been recog-nized, as may be observed in the following citation from a classical grammar: "The construc-tion of conditional sentences in MH follows in the main the principles of similar sentences in BH" (M. H. Segal, *A Grammar of Mishnaic Hebrew* [Oxford: Clarendon, 1927] 227.) The comprehensive discussion of the syntax of conditional sentences that follows (pp. 227–31) makes no reference whatsoever to the biblical norm of marking a legal protasis with כי. Simi-larly, Qimron provides a valuable analysis of the trend at Qumran to prefer the future perfect in a protasis (קטל + אם) over the biblical norm, which more frequently employs the imperfect (יקטל + אם); see idem, *Hebrew of the Dead Sea Scrolls*, 84–85. This analysis, however, does not mention casuistic law. Nor does it refer to a more striking change in the construction of conditional sentences: the widespread loss at Qumran of [יקטל + כי] as marking the protasis, although that formulation was standard in Biblical Hebrew. That classical construction is preserved at Qumran primarily in biblical texts or in rewritten biblical material and, even then, not always consistently.

41. "Rewritten Scripture" texts such as the Reworked Pentateuch (4Q158; 4Q364–367) are here classified as biblical texts, since their use of conditional כי is a function of its occurrence in the biblical text they are expanding; it does not represent an independent use.

Scroll's retention of the conditional just as anomalous as its replacement by אם. From the perspective of Qumran Hebrew, the Temple Scroll should not have retained כי at all. From the perspective of its biblical *Vorlagen* and other rewritten Scripture texts like 4QRP, it should have retained every כי. It is the simultaneous departure from both norms, virtually unique to the Temple Scroll, that requires explanation. The uniqueness of the phenomenon, in turn, demands that any proposed explanation be equally text-specific. What is there about the Temple Scroll as a text that makes *both* the replacement *and* the retention of כי a distinctive feature of its discourse?

No merely mechanical solution to this problem is possible. The widely accepted source-critical analysis of the Temple Scroll cannot account for the replacements.[42] The change cuts across the boundaries of these proposed sources, which rules out a scenario in which one source used כי and another used אם.[43] Nor does the fact that MS A of the Temple Scroll (11Q19) was written by two different scribes explain the distribution of the change. Whereas the replacement occurs in cols. 43–61, only cols. 2–5 stem from the second scribal hand.[44] Accordingly, the replacement operates neither at the level of any of the possible sources nor at the level of those who copied the scroll. The substitution is, to the contrary, part and parcel of the compositional strategies of the Temple Scroll's redactor. In

---

42. The initial argument for literary sources within the Temple Scroll by Wilson and Wills has been extended, with some modifications, by Michael Wise; see Andrew M. Wilson and Lawrence Wills, "Literary Sources of the Temple Scroll," *HTR* 75 (1982) 275–88; and Michael O. Wise, *A Critical Study of the Temple Scroll from Cave 11* (SAOC 49; Chicago: University of Chicago Press, 1990). Sidnie White Crawford demonstrates the extent to which this source-critical model has permeated scholarship, in *The Temple Scroll and Related Texts* (Companion to the Qumran Scrolls 2; Sheffield: Sheffield Academic Press, 2000) 22–24, 34–62. While the likelihood that the Temple Scroll incorporates earlier nonbiblical as well as biblical material should not be denied, attempts to reconstruct these sources on the basis of alleged stylistic and compositional peculiarities fail to consider the complex relationship between the Temple Scroll and its biblical sources. Astutely questioning the source-critical approach before it was even suggested is Steven A. Kaufman, "The Temple Scroll and Higher Criticism," *HUCA* 53 (1982) 29–43. For a different approach, see Molly M. Zahn, "Schneiderei oder Weberei: Zum Verständnis der Diachronie der Tempelrolle," *RevQ* 20 (2001) 255–86; and eadem, "4QReworked Pentateuch C and the Literary Sources of the *Temple Scroll*: A New (Old) Proposal," *DSD* 19 (2012) 133–58.

43. The change in 11QTemple 43:13 occurs within Wilson and Wills's "Temple and Courts" source (= Wise's "Temple Source"). The change in 11QTemple 58:15 is part of the Law of the King (cols. 57–59). The rest of the replacements occur within the reworked Deuteronomic material (Wise's "Deuteronomy Source"; roughly cols. 51–56 and 60–66). Most of the retentions of כי also occur in the Deuteronomy Source. That כי is both replaced and retained so often within a single proposed source confirms that the problem cannot be solved source-critically.

44. Yadin, *Temple Scroll*, 1:11–12, 17–20.

order to explain the phenomenon, therefore, one must connect the question of language to the question of the text.

III. The Connection between Syntax and Text

The composer of the Temple Scroll was trying to present his community with a coherent system of law for an ideal Israel dominated by an ideal Temple.[45] Alongside the extensive construction plan (cols. 3–13, 30–47), he included large sections of legal material that intertwine biblical law with nonbiblical legal exegesis (cols. 14–29, 48–66). But the redactor did not reuse the biblical text passively. He worked to smooth it out by clarifying or reinterpreting difficult passages, by harmonizing conflicting prescriptions, and by bringing together thematically related laws.[46] The need to redact in these ways was triggered by the nature of biblical law itself. The canonical Pentateuch is a highly redacted work that includes three mutually independent and mutually inconsistent legal collections, written at diverse times, each distinguished by its own system of language and priorities. The inevitable result is a text full of inconsistencies, contradictions, and repetitions. Seen from this perspective, the Temple Scroll is more than the blueprint for a more perfect Temple. It also represents the attempt to create a more perfect Torah: a Torah that is self-consistent and clearly organized. If the measurements of the Temple are ideally conceived, the arrangement of the Temple Scroll as its religious-legal blueprint reflects a corresponding concern with textual draftsmanship.[47]

That redactional project is enhanced by the Temple Scroll's theonymous attribution.[48] The scroll presents itself as being spoken directly by

---

45. This is pointed out clearly by Lawrence H. Schiffman, "The Deuteronomic Paraphrase of the *Temple Scroll*," *RevQ* 15 (1991) 543–67 (esp. p. 545).

46. See Yadin, *Temple Scroll*, 1:71–88.

47. The Temple Scroll was not the only work of the Second Temple period to rearrange biblical law in the service of a more systematically organized legal exegesis. See David Altshuler, "On the Classification of Judaic Laws in the *Antiquities* of Josephus and the Temple Scroll of Qumran," *AJSReview* 7–8 (1982–83) 1–14.

48. See Yadin, *Temple Scroll*, 1:82 n. 76, 87, 390–92 (esp. p. 390 n. 8). For important reassessments, see Moshe J. Bernstein, "Pseudepigraphy in the Qumran Scrolls: Categories and Functions," in *Pseudepigraphic Perspectives: The Apocrypha and Pseudepigrapha in Light of the Dead Sea Scrolls* (ed. Esther G. Chazon and Michael Stone; STDJ 31; Leiden: Brill, 1999) 1–26 (esp. pp. 13–17); and Lawrence H. Schiffman, "The Temple Scroll and the Halakhic Pseudepigrapha of the Second Temple Period," in *Pseudepigraphic Perspectives: The Apocrypha and Pseudepigrapha in Light of the Dead Sea Scrolls* (ed. Esther G. Chazon and Michael Stone; STDJ 31; Leiden: Brill, 1999) 121–31.

God to Moses on Mt. Sinai.[49] With this bid for its own authority, the Temple Scroll competes with and seeks to trump the Pentateuch as well as other Second Temple works that claim, directly or indirectly, to be revealed. The revelation contained in the Temple Scroll, spoken directly by God, is presented as immediate, while the canonical Pentateuch presents only a mediated revelation spoken by Moses. In *Jubilees*, an angel reports God's words to Moses; God does not speak directly.[50]

There is a profound connection between the voicing and the redactor's editorial activity that has not previously been seen. More conventionally, the Temple Scroll's voicing has been discussed separately from its reinterpretation and rearrangement of the biblical text. This implies that the divine attribution was merely a final veneer designed to embellish and authorize the halakic exegesis of the text. We contend that the systemization of biblical law complements the text's voicing and constitutes a crucial aspect of the scroll's authority claim. The re-editing of the Pentateuch by the redactor of the Temple Scroll represents an attempt to "de-edit" Torah. By removing the repetitions and logical inconsistencies that stem from the highly redacted nature of the canonical Pentateuch, by increasing the text's coherence and consistency, the redactor presents a more perfect Torah—one more worthy of God.[51] If redaction is a sign of human handiwork, then the goal of the Temple Scroll's redactor is to offer his community a legal revelation unmarred by human handiwork. The move against the canonical Pentateuch is thus twofold: the Temple Scroll attempts to supersede the Pentateuch, first, by presenting itself as unmediated revelation and, second, by undoing the work of the pentateuchal redactor in the attempt to create a more coherent, "de-edited" Torah.

This hermeneutical project of the redactor permeates the text even to the level of the choice of conditionals. Language itself becomes a tool that

---

49. The deliberate presentation of the scroll as spoken by God is made clear by the systematic change in voicing when the redactor reuses material from Deuteronomy. There, because Moses is the speaker, references to God are in the third person. In the Temple Scroll, these references are recast in the first person to make God the speaker. See Yadin, *Temple Scroll*, 1:71–72.

50. See Hindy Najman, "Interpretation as Primordial Writing: Jubilees and Its Authority Conferring Strategies," *JSJ* 30 (1999) 379–410.

51. From the standpoint of the history of religions, "unicity" is a defining characteristic of texts holding the status of Scripture; see William A. Graham, "Scripture," in *The Encyclopedia of Religion* (ed. Mircea Eliade; 16 vols.; New York: Macmillan, 1987) 13:133–45 (at p. 141). This model, however, does not take into account the hermeneutical issues encountered by Second Temple readers as they confronted the highly redacted Pentateuch, with its redundant and inconsistent laws and narratives. From this perspective, texts like the Temple Scroll and *Jubilees* represent the attempt to create unicity exegetically by reordering and rewriting the Pentateuch.

can be wielded to advance compositional goals. Within the context of the Temple Scroll's editorial "de-editing" of the Torah, the conditionals present a unique problem. Although the redactor's project of bringing together like materials contributed to the creation of a more organized text, it simultaneously intensified the conflict between source texts, since, by definition, each pentateuchal source is distinguished by its own distinct vocabulary and legal formulations. In this way, the reordering used to accomplish the first goal—a coherent halakic system—risked undercutting the second goal—the consistency of divine voicing—if the editorial seams became too obvious. The redactor did not have a problem with different legal structures and vocabularies per se, since in general he preserved the language of his various source materials. But the conditional particles demanded special attention. The alternation of laws marked by classical כי with those marked by vernacular אם in texts newly brought into conjunction by the editing process would disrupt the fiction of coherent divine speech.

The simplest and most cohesive solution would be to omit כי altogether: to level *every* occurrence of כי to אם as a way of smoothing the editorial seams between sections of casuistic law. This would represent the ultimate "de-editing" of the text: the consistent use of only one instead of two semantically identical conditional particles. But the redactor was simultaneously pulled in another direction. His attempt to place the text on a par with Scripture also entailed the attempt to imitate biblical language.[52] Precisely the historically distant, conditional use of כי distinguished the classical literary language of biblical law: כי had to be used in order to give the text the patina of Scripture. Torah without כי would not be "biblical."[53]

---

52. For the argument that many of the distinctive linguistic features attested in the DSS do not preserve a vernacular but point to the conscious cultivation of a "scriptural" language (based on hyperarchaisms, such as lengthened pronouns and the routine use of pausal forms and cohortatives), see William M. Schniedewind, "Qumran Hebrew as an Antilanguage," *JBL* 118 (1999) 235–52; and idem, "Linguistic Ideology in Qumran Hebrew," in *Diggers at the Well: Proceedings of a Third International Symposium on the Hebrew of the Dead Sea Scrolls and Ben Sira* (ed. Takamitsu Muraoka and John F. Elwolde; STDJ 36; Leiden: Brill, 2000) 245–55. This very productive model should also distinguish language use in different types of texts and genres, as Steve Weitzman notes in his own fine study of the language ideology of the DSS ("Why Did the Qumran Community Write in Hebrew?" *JAOS* 119 [1999] 35–45).

53. Similarly, the King James (Authorized) Version (1611) won such prestige within American Protestantism that, in effect, it defined "Scripture." Its English rendering was deemed "inerrant," as were also its punctuation and use of italics. When liberal Protestantism attempted a more modern translation that was informed by biblical scholarship—the Revised Standard Version (1952)—many quarters of conservative Protestantism rejected it as nonbiblical and heretical. Faced with this serious threat, the American Air Force Reserves cautioned against the new translation. See Peter J. Thuesen, *In Discordance with the Scriptures: American Protestant Battles over Translating the Bible* (Oxford: Oxford University Press, 1999) 50–51, 108–9.

It would ring just as false in the ears of the redactor and his community as would Shakespeare, for a later audience, without "thee" and "thou." The redactor's goals thus came into conflict with one another: the very desire to write biblically—which required כי—paradoxically interfered with the redactor's commitment to produce a coherent revelation of law spoken by a coherent God.

IV. The Significance of the Manuscript's Spacing System

Since כי was an essential component of classical biblical law, the question became how to make sense of this outdated conditional that nonetheless needed to be used. The redactor of the Temple Scroll devised a consistent system governing the use or nonuse of כי. We have determined that there is a definite correlation between the choice of conditional and the manuscript's formal system of spacing or intervals.[54] In the Temple Scroll, all appearances of conditional כי that occur in the middle of a line

---

54. Dividing a text into logical units by means of spacing was the norm in both biblical and nonbiblical texts from Qumran. The system is analogous to the later Masoretic system of *pārāšiyyôt*, employing open and closed paragraph markers (פתוחה and סתומה) as the basic sense divisions. Given the use of various sense divisions in Akkadian, Ugaritic, Phoenician, Aramaic, and Greek texts of the second and especially the first millennium B.C.E., some form of spacing system may already have been present in the biblical texts at the time of their composition. See Emanuel Tov, "The Background of the Sense Divisions in the Biblical Texts," in *Delimitation Criticism: A New Tool in Biblical Scholarship* (ed. Marjo C. A. Korpel and Josef M. Oesch; Pericope 1; Assen: Van Gorcum, 2000) 312–50 (at pp. 334–35). In their contributions to the same volume, while valuably demonstrating the antiquity and importance of the manuscript spacing system, Korpel and Oesch express confidence in being able to recover the spacing divisions original to the autographs of biblical manuscripts (Korpel, 1–50 [at p. 10]; and Oesch, 197–229 [at pp. 219–22]). This sort of confidence seems excessive, especially since what is to be recovered is, after all, only hypothetically present in the first place (note also the reservations of Tov, "Background of the Sense Divisions," 337). Moreover, Syro-Palestinian inscriptional evidence and the limited corpus in paleo-Hebrew must also be taken into account. This material often appears only with occasional word dividers rather than with any formal system of spacing (as on the Moabite Stone). These same issues arise in the earlier study by Oesch, *Petuchah und Setumah: Untersuchungen zu einer überlieferten Gliederung im hebräischen Text des Alten Testaments* (OBO 27; Göttingen: Vandenhoeck & Ruprecht, 1979) 348–49, 364. Previously noting the correspondences between the Qumran and MT systems are: Ernst Würthwein, *The Text of the Old Testament* (Grand Rapids: Eerdmans, 1979) 20–21; Shemaryahu Talmon, "Aspects of the Textual Transmission of the Bible in the Light of Qumran Manuscripts," in *Qumran and the History of the Biblical Text* (ed. Frank Moore Cross and Shemaryahu Talmon; Cambridge: Harvard University Press, 1975) 226–63 (at p. 227); Emanuel Tov, "The Orthography and Language of the Hebrew Scrolls Found at Qumran and the Origin of These Scrolls," *Textus* 13 (1986) 31–37; idem, "Hebrew Biblical Manuscripts from the Judean Desert: Their Contribution to Textual Criticism," *JJS* 39 (1988) 5–37; and idem, *Textual Criticism of the Hebrew Bible* (2nd ed.; Minneapolis: Fortress / Assen: Van Gorcum, 2001) 195–96, 198–200.

are preceded by a larger-than-normal interval.[55] When conditional כי appears at the beginning of a line, most often the previous line ends with an interval.[56] In three exceptional cases, the previous line runs to the left margin.[57] (The data, in the form of a complete map of the use of conditionals in 11QT[a], follow in appendix 2, pp. 102–106).

Conditional כי in the Temple Scroll is nearly always preceded by what, in the Masoretic system, would be defined as a closed paragraph interval (סתומה) or an open paragraph interval (פתוחה).[58] In effect, conditional כי was restricted to a specific function in the Temple Scroll: it marked the beginning of a new unit of law. [59] The redactor's consistent insertion of an interval before כי is more systematic than in the system of סתומה and פתוחה in the MT or the קצה system of the Samaritan Pentateuch (SP): the Temple Scroll on several occasions inserts an interval before כי in places where the MT and SP do not preserve a paragraph marker.[60]

---

55. The larger interval is attested 12 times (11QTemple 45:7; 53:14, 16; 60:12; 61:2, 12; 62:5; 64:6, 9; 65:5, 7; 66:8).

56. The interval at the end of the line occurs seven times (11QTemple 49:5; 50:10; 56:12; 58:3; 60:16; 63:10; 64:2). This analysis includes all instances where כי marks a protasis, both in its prevailing use as "if" and in its temporal use as "when." The temporal use occurs in the Temple Scroll only twice. Both appearances are where the Temple Scroll reproduces Deuteronomy's "land-grant formula" ("When you enter the land . . ."), which cannot carry a conditional meaning although it takes the same syntactical form (11QTemple 56:12 = Deut 17:14; 11QTemple 60:16 = Deut 18:9). On the *Landgabeformel*, see Norbert Lohfink, *Studien zum Deuteronomium und zur deuteronomistischen Literatur II* (SBAB 12; Stuttgart: Katholisches Bibelwerk, 1991) 125–42.

57. 11QTemple 45:11; 53:11; 58:10. Note that in the second and third cases, the protasis marker is the redundant double conditional וכי אם (see §VII below).

58. For a clear exposition of the Masoretic system, see Israel Yeivin, *Introduction to the Tiberian Masorah* (SBLMasS 5; Chico, CA: Scholars Press, 1979) 39–43.

59. This strict correlation between the spacing system and the use of the conditional is specific to 11QTemple[a]. It does not apply consistently, for example, to 4Q158. At the same time, whether the latter actually had an organized system of spacing is difficult to determine because of the text's fragmentary preservation. Compounding the difficulty is the failure of the official edition of 4Q158 to represent the manuscript's spacing system accurately and consistently. Allegro's transcription (*Qumran Cave 4* [DJD 5] 4) omits, for example, the interval set in the manuscript before the conditional וכי at 4Q158 frg. 11, line 6 (= כי in MT Exod 22:4), although it is very clear in plate I, frg. 11. This interval corresponds to the closed paragraph set before the same conditional in the MT. Two lines farther down, however, no interval appears before the next law's protasis marker, כיא (= כי in MT Exod 22:6), where, again, the MT does have an interval of this sort (closed paragraph). Here the transcription is correct (ibid., p. 5, frg. 11, line 9; corresponding to plate I, frg. 11). The scribe set a large interval before Exod 21:1, which is the superscription to the Covenant Code (4Q158, frg. 7, line 9; correctly, ibid., p. 4; and plate I). The MT also marks this with a major interval (open paragraph) since the verse begins a new lection (*pārāšāh*).

60. In three instances, there is a space in the Temple Scroll but not in the MT (11QTemple 53:14 = Num 30:3; 53:16 = Num 30:4; and 61:2 = Deut 18:21). In six instances, the scroll has a space where the SP has none (the preceding three, and 11QTemple 60:12 =

The tight regulation of conditional כי sharply contrasts with the situation of אם. While אם may be used after an interval, it also occurs frequently with no preceding interval.[61] In other words, אם *could* fulfill the same introductory function as כי, but it had a wider range of uses and was not as restricted. The special regulation of כי and the lack of regulation of אם most likely reflect the linguistic situation of the redactor: while the classical conditional use of כי was obsolete and foreign in the late Second Temple period and thus required special attention to control its use, the conditional meaning of vernacular אם was unambiguous, whether it marked the beginning of a unit or occurred within a unit.

This map of the text makes it possible to determine when a biblical source text formulated in כי might be "translated" into אם. A complex array of forces lay behind the replacement. As the desire to produce a systematic text competed with the desire to mimic biblical legal syntax, the redactor devised a system to regulate the use of conditional כי precisely because it had become a scriptural fossil. Given the complex task faced by the editor, it is not surprising that there are two distinct situations in which the substitution occurs. Recalling the redactor's larger goal of constructing a coherent re-redaction of legal exegesis, consistently attributed to God, the first and simplest trigger is the desire for redactional smoothing. The second trigger represents the other side of the coin: the redactor's push for systemization by strictly regulating the use of כי. Each of the two contexts for the change represents a different implementation of the redactor's overarching hermeneutical program.

V. Redactional Smoothing
as the First Trigger for the Substitution

Six of the ten replacements occur where the redactor has set source material that contains protases beginning with כי directly following a section of text that contains protases beginning with אם. Following the literary model of the first set of laws, the redactor changes כי in the following section to אם. By unifying the legal language, he smooths the redactional seam between the two texts, eliminating the telltale inconsistency of conditional markers that points to his having combined two originally separate

---

Deut 18:6; 60:21 = Deut 18:14; 65:5 = Deut 22:8). Note that the כי in 11QTemple 60:21 represents causal "for" rather than conditional "if," despite the interval that precedes it.

61. The word אם occurs with an interval 9 times (11QTemple 15:15; 53:19; 54:8, 19; 55:2, 15; 58:11, 15; 59:16) and without an interval 18 times (11QTemple 43:13; 47:15, 16; 50:7, 12; 52:9; 53:11, 12; 55:13; 57:18; 58:6, 7, 10; 61:7; 62:6, 8; 64:14; 66:4).

sources. Leveling the conditionals gives the appearance of a coherent text, as befits writing that claims to be divinely revealed.

The phenomenon occurs in two sections of the Temple Scroll. In the first, following the extended reproduction of the laws of vows from Numbers 30, the redactor inserts the series of apostasy laws from Deuteronomy 13 and 17. The section on vows in Num 30:3–17 contains seven sub-conditions with אם.[62] In contrast, the Deuteronomic apostasy laws begin consistently with כי (Deut 13:2, 7, 13; 17:2). The redactor aligns the protasis markers of the laws taken from Deuteronomy so that they conform to the markers in Numbers, thereby creating a single block of now-consistent laws:

Biblical Source	Original Form	Form in Temple Scroll	11QTemple
Num 30:3	איש כי	ואיש כי	53:14
Num 30:4	ואשה כי	ואשה כי	53:16
Num 30:6	ואם	ואם	53:19
Num 30:7	ואם	[ואם]	54:0?
Num 30:9	ואם	[ואם]	54:0?
Num 30:11	ואם	[ואם]	54:0?
Num 30:13	ואם	[ואם]	54:0?
Num 30:15	ואם	[ואם]	54:0?
Num 30:16	ואם	ואם	54:1
Deut 13:2	כי	אם	54:8
Deut 13:7	כי	ואם	54:19
Deut 13:13	כי	אם	55:2
Deut 13:19	כי	אם	55:13
Deut 17:2	כי	אם	55:15

FIGURE 1.3. Replacement in Order to Smooth Redactional Seams

A similar situation appears in part of the scroll's Law of the King (11QT 56:12–59:21). Column 58 presents an ordered series of military situations

---

62. Num 30:6, 7, 9, 11, 13, 15, 16. Only two of these are extant in the Temple Scroll (11QT 53:19; 54:1). However, the first seven lines of col. 54 have not been preserved. It is virtually certain that those lines originally continued, with some adjustments, from Num 30:6, where col. 53 ends, to Num 30:16, where the legible portions of col. 54 begin (see Yadin, *Temple Scroll*, 2:241).

and prescribes the response of the monarch as commander in chief in each case. The cases are consistently introduced with אם (11QT 58:6, 7, 11). After several examples, each with אם, that lack direct biblical basis, the redactor includes a clause that is closely based on one of the Deuteronomic war laws: כִּי תֵצֵא לַמִּלְחָמָה עַל אֹיְבֶיךָ, "If you go out to war against your enemies" (Deut 20:1). But, in introducing the lemma into its new context, he revises it in two ways. The opening כי of Deuteronomy is changed to אם, and the lemma is recast in the third person, וְאִם יֵצֵא לַמִּלְחָמָה עַל אֹיְבָיו, "If he goes out to war against his enemies" (11QT 58:15). These changes not only make the protasis marker consistent with the previous section, obscuring the insertion of material from a different source, but also bring it into grammatical conformity with the rest of the section, in which the king is the grammatical subject. As a result, the biblical textual source is assimilated to its new context. At the same time, a radical revision of biblical law is obscured: Deuteronomy's war laws make no mention of the monarch, an arguably deliberate silence with the intention of restricting the king's military powers.[63]

VI. The Inconsistent Use of כי in the Pentateuch as the Second Trigger for the Substitution

The second trigger reflects the redactor's recognition that the legal corpora of the Pentateuch are inconsistent in their use of conditional כי and his desire, nonetheless, to maintain the consistency of his own system. Because it represents a combination of diverse legal corpora, the Pentateuch is correspondingly diverse in its legal syntax.[64] The casuistic laws of the Covenant Code (i.e., Exod 21:2–22:16) employ a distinctive system for demarcating units and for distinguishing between main clause

---

63. See Bernard M. Levinson, "The Reconceptualization of Kingship in Deuteronomy and the Deuteronomistic History's Transformation of Torah," *VT* 51 (2001) 511–34.

64. The three different legal collections normally recognized by scholars are the Covenant Code (Exodus 21–23), the legal corpus of Deuteronomy 12–26, and the Holiness Code (Leviticus 17–26). Separate from these three legal collections are additional laws that are scattered throughout the Pentateuch, particularly in the Priestly source. The first section of the Covenant Code (Exod 21:2–22:16) is composed primarily of casuistic laws. This section, normally regarded as the most ancient, is the focus of the discussion here. Following the primarily casuistic block of civil and criminal laws are laws that have both a different focus (ethical laws appealing to conscience; religious and cultic laws) and a different formulation (apodictic; casuistic laws in the second person). For an overview of attempts to explain this range of forms as reflecting literary and redactional history, see Bernard M. Levinson, ed., *Theory and Method in Biblical and Cuneiform Law: Revision, Interpolation, and Development* (JSOTSup 181; Sheffield: Sheffield Academic Press, 1994; repr., Classic Reprints, Sheffield: Phoenix, 2006).

and subconditions that may be termed "the hierarchical ordering of conditionals." The main law is consistently marked by conditional כי, while אם marks the subconditions.[65] The operation of this system is best shown graphically. Thus fig. 1.4 shows the Covenant Code's two separate laws concerned with the manumission of slaves (Exod 21:2–6, 7–12).[66]

Exodus 21 *Verse*	*Structure of Apodosis*	*Protasis Marker ("If")*		
		Subcondition	*Main Condition*	
2	שש שנים יעבד . . . <u>יצא</u> לחפשי חנם		כי	A
3a	<u>יצא</u>	אם$_1$		
3b	<u>ויצאה</u>	אם$_2$		
4	<u>יצא</u>	אם$_3$		
5–6	<u>לא אצא</u> חפשי . . . ועבדו לעלם	ואם$_4$		B
7	<u>לא תצא</u> כצאת העבדים		וכי	B
8		אם$_1$		
9		ואם$_2$		
10		אם$_3$		
11	<u>ויצאה</u> חנם אין כסף	ואם$_4$		A

FIGURE 1.4. Hierarchical Ordering of Conditionals in the Covenant Code (The Laws of Manumission)

65. For a valuable summary and analysis of the relevant literature, see Shalom M. Paul, *Studies in the Book of the Covenant in the Light of Cuneiform and Biblical Law* (VTSup 18; Leiden: Brill, 1970) 112–18. While the term "hierarchical ordering of conditionals" has not, as far as we know, been used previously, the different roles assigned to the two particles have previously been seen. One of the first detailed studies was by Alfred Jepsen, *Untersuchungen zum Bundesbuch* (BWANT 3/5; Stuttgart: Kohlhammer, 1927). A comprehensive analysis was also attempted by Gerhard Liedke, *Gestalt und Bezeichnung alttestamentlicher Rechtssätze: Eine formgeschichtlich-terminologische Studie* (WMANT 39; Neukirchen-Vluyn: Neukirchener Verlag, 1971) 31–34. See further Yuichi Osumi, *Die Kompositionsgeschichte des Bundesbuches Exodus 20,22b–23,3* (OBO 105; Freiburg: Universitätsverlag / Göttingen: Vandenhoeck & Ruprecht, 1991) 93–101.

66. The following diagram builds on the valuable model provided by Norbert Lohfink, "Fortschreibung? Zur Technik vom Rechtsrevisionen im deuteronomischen Bereich, erörtert an Deuteronomium 12, Ex 21,2–11 und Dtn 15,12–18," in *Studien zum Deuteronomium und zur deuteronomistichen Literatur, IV* (SBAB 31; Stuttgart: Katholisches Bibelwerk, 2000) 163–203 (at p. 188).

Despite their semantic equivalence, the two conditionals are not interchangeable: they occur in a fixed and highly regulated sequence. The first כִּי introduces the law concerned with male slaves; each אִם that follows addresses complications and variations of this law. The return to כִּי marks a new law devoted to female slaves.[67] In effect, therefore, conditional כִּי plays a double role. It marks a "new law," defining the beginning of the unit, as much as it marks the protasis. The shared topic of both laws is the interrelation between property law (slavery and indenture) and family law (marriage, children, inheritance). The two main clauses (marked by כִּי) divide this boundary area into two categories based on gender. The sub-clauses (marked by אִם) introduce further permutations, exploring binary distinctions: ± marriage, ± children, ± manumission.

The system's highly structured, carefully ordered analysis of gender, property, and family law points to the intellectual culture of the scribal schools as the context for this sort of legal and literary draftsmanship.[68] The hierarchical ordering of the conditionals throughout the casuistic section of the Covenant Code constitutes further evidence of this ancient Near Eastern scribal heritage.[69] A similar distinction between conditionals

---

67. The structural symmetry between these two laws disproves Liedke's claim that there is a functional distinction between וְאִם and אִם, and thus the form with the copula marks a sub-subcondition (*Alttestamentlicher Rechtssätze*, 32–33).

68. See Eckart Otto, *Körperverletzungen in den Keilschriftrechten und im Alten Testament: Studien zum Rechtstransfer im Alten Orient* (AOAT 226; Kevelaer: Butzon & Bercker / Neukirchen-Vluyn: Neukirchener Verlag, 1991) 175.

69. Unaware of Bandstra's dissertation (see n. 17 above), Aejmelaeus similarly notes that, in determining the meaning of כִּי, it is important to determine whether the clause with the particle precedes or follows the main clause ("Function and Interpretation," 170; see n. 15 above). The subsequent move to subsume all fronted clauses under the single category "circumstantial" (ibid., 170–71), however, does scant justice to cases of highly regulated, genre-specific use, as in casuistic law, which assigns distinct functions to both כִּי and אִם. Moreover, the distinction between the clauses introduced by each is not simply the degree of "individual detail" (ibid., 170 n. 10). Rather, the two particles distinguish between main condition and subcondition (see, correctly, Schoors, "Particle כִּי," 270). A similar error provides the point of departure for a brief discussion of the distinction between כִּי and אִם in Follingstad (*Deictic Viewpoint*, 268–72). Seeking to summarize the standard scholarly view, Follingstad claims that כִּי marks "major" laws, while אִם marks "minor" laws (p. 268). Were that the case, one could imagine a minor law (say, concerning procedure rather than governing an actual delict) being found independent of a major law; yet this is never the case in the casuistic section of the Covenant Code, where all אִם laws are nested within a legal unit defined by an initial כִּי; they occur in fixed sequence. In fairness, it is not clear that the error in the point of departure has any bearing on what follows, since the author proceeds immediately to propose a different theory about the function of the two particles—a theory that makes no reference either to the previous theory or to law. It seems to be presented as a general rule valid for BH, without generic restriction. Based on a rather small statistical sample—Josh 24:20—the author claims that כִּי marks protases in which the speaker is uncommitted to the truth of his utterance, whereas אִם assumes such commitment. This hypothesis is not clearly demonstrated

is evident in the Hittite laws.[70] The Ugaritic hippiatric corpus, which employs the casuistic form to systematize veterinary medicine, also attests this system.[71] This corpus provides important evidence, independent of the genre of law, for the spread of Mesopotamian scientific literature into the area of Syria–Palestine and into Northwest Semitic.[72] The Laws of Hammurabi also similarly distinguishes between primary and subordinate clauses but distinguishes them by the verbal form rather than the conditional conjunction.[73]

Deuteronomy significantly modified the older system represented by the Covenant Code. The innovations in religion and law that make Deuteronomy distinctive took place through the authors' engagement with a range of both Israelite and Near Eastern literary genres, the legal genre being primary.[74] In this scribal context, the authors of Deuteronomy also

---

with respect to the operation of conditionals elsewhere in the same chapter (note the sequence of three אם clauses in Josh 24:15), in other narrative texts, or in legal texts. Indeed, the rationale for the new theory altogether remains unclear, since there is no critique of the one cited in reference to law, while the alternative is not presented as valid only for narrative.

70. In the Hittite Laws, the main condition, or protasis, is "introduced by *takku* 'if,'" and the subordinate one by *mān* 'if/when.'" The subordinate clauses so marked, as in §§8, 10, arise at the level of the New Hittite revision (1400–1180 B.C.E.) of the Old Hittite version with simple protasis; see Harry A. Hoffner, *The Laws of the Hittites: A Critical Edition* (DMOA 23; Leiden: Brill, 1997) 12.

71. In the Ugaritic Hippiatric corpus, *k* (or *w . k*) introduces the main conditional clause: a distinct medical case describing an illness from which a horse might suffer (RS 17:120, lines 1, 5, 7, 9, 12, 15, 18, 20, 23, 30). In contrast, *hm*, "if," never marks the main "condition." Instead, coordinated as *hm . . . hm*, "either . . . or" (thus corresponding to Akkadian *lū . . . lū*), it marks secondary subordinate clauses, prescribing alternate courses of treatment (RS 17:120, lines 3–4). For the citations from Tablet 1 just given, see Cohen and Sivan, *Ugaritic Hippiatric Texts*, 9; and Pardee, *Les Textes Hippiatriques*, 21–23. Pardee recognizes that the hierarchical sequence *k . . . hm* corresponds precisely to Hebrew אם . . . כי (ibid., 41).

72. On the scholarly nature of this corpus, see Dennis Pardee, "Ugaritic Science," in *The World of the Aramaeans: Studies in Language and Literature in Honour of Paul-Eugène Dion* (ed. P. M. Michèle Daviau, John W. Wevers, and Michael Weigl; 3 vols.; JSOTSup 324–326; Sheffield: Sheffield Academic Press, 2001) 3:223–54.

73. The main clause was marked by *šumma* ("if") + preterite, while subconditions were marked by *šumma* + perfect; thus, the main law beginning with the preterite in Laws of Hammurabi §17 is followed by subconditions formulated in the perfect in §§18–20. The beginning of a new legal unit is marked by the return to the preterite in §21. This technique of using different verb forms to specify the relationship *between* legal protases seems to have been overlooked in the major grammars. The switch from preterite to perfect to mark the final clause(s) of a compound protasis is, however, clearly noted. See Wolfram von Soden with Werner R. Mayer, *Grundriss der Akkadischen Grammatik* (3rd ed.; AnOr 33; Rome: Pontifical Biblical Institute, 1995) 261 (§161e); John Huehnergard, *A Grammar of Akkadian* (HSM 45; Atlanta: Scholars Press, 1996) 157 (§17.2); and Martha T. Roth, ed., *Law Collections from Mesopotamia and Asia Minor* (2nd ed.; SBLWAW 6; Atlanta: Scholars Press, 1997) 8.

74. On Deuteronomy's transformation of prior Israelite religion and law, see Bernard M. Levinson, *Deuteronomy and the Hermeneutics of Legal Innovation* (Oxford: Oxford University Press, 1997); and Eckart Otto, *Das Deuteronomium: Politische Theologie und Rechts-*

developed new forms of speech and writing; their distinctive literary and rhetorical style came to be emulated by a wide range of subsequent Israel-ite authors and editors.[75] One particular development by Deuteronomy's scribes that apprently has never previously been identified involves a new way of defining a legal unit. Whereas in the Covenant Code conditional כי was restricted to marking a new legal paragraph, the same term was given an additional function in the legal corpus of Deuteronomy: here it could also mark a subordinate clause. For example, Deuteronomy's firstlings law begins with the apodictic requirement: כל הבכור אשר יולד בקרבך ובצאנך הזכר תקדיש ליהוה אלהיך, "Every male firstling that is born among your cattle or among your sheep you shall consecrate to Yahweh your God" (Deut 15:19).

Immediately following this general statement, the authors of Deuter-onomy excluded certain animals from this requirement. This exception was introduced with a כי clause: וכי יהיה בו מום פסח או עור כל מום רע לא תזבחנו ליהוה אלהיך, "*But if* it has a defect of lameness or blindness, any serious defect, you shall not sacrifice it to Yahweh your God" (Deut 15:21). In marking a subcondition of the already-introduced main case, כי has here assumed precisely the function that was assigned to אם in the Covenant Code.[76] Conversely, in the Covenant Code, the "new unit marker" would have been כי, whereas the firstlings law of Deuteronomy begins with an

---

reform in Juda und Assyrien (BZAW 284; Berlin: de Gruyter, 1999). Deuteronomy's interac-tion with cuneiform literary material helps account for specific details of language, topos, and formulation. For a specific example, see Bernard M. Levinson, "Textual Criticism, As-syriology, and the History of Interpretation: Deuteronomy 13:7a as a Test Case in Method," *"The Right Chorale": Studies in Biblical Law and Interpretation* (FAT 54; Tübingen: Mohr Siebeck, 2008) 112–44.

75. See the important analysis of Moshe Weinfeld, *Deuteronomy and the Deuteronomic School* (Oxford: Clarendon, 1972) 171–78, 320–65.

76. The attempt to impose a single model for the use of כי on the Pentateuch and thus to subsume Deuteronomy into the Covenant Code leads to serious distortions in the exegesis of the text. For example, by assuming that the conditional in Deuteronomy auto-matically has the same function of marking a new law that it has in the Covenant Code, sev-eral scholars conclude that Deuteronomy's manumission law (Deut 15:12–18) is composed of three separate "main cases" (at vv. 12, 13, 16), despite the fact that it more logically follows the literary model of the single law for manumission found in the Covenant Code (Exod 21:2–6). See Liedke, *Alttestamentliche Rechtssätze*, 32; and, following Liedke's analysis, is Gregory C. Chirichigno, *Debt-Slavery in Israel and the Ancient Near East* (JSOTSup 141; Sheffield: Shef-field Academic Press, 1993) 262. However, Schoors ("Particle כי," 271) correctly sees that Deuteronomy thus expands the function of כי, employing it in ways that the Covenant Code would have reserved for אם (in relation to Deut 15:13, 16). Lohfink similarly challenges Liedke and Chirichigno on this point ("Fortschreibung," 192 n. 9, 195 n. 102). However, as will be demonstrated, while Deut 15:12 should be read as a new conditional law, v. 13 should be read as a temporal clause rather than a subcondition; and the grammatical construction of the possible subcondition at v. 16 (והיה כי) is anomalous. See part 2, pp. 65–74.

apodictic general rule. This new system of defining a legal unit is represented graphically in fig. 1.5.

	If Main Clause Is Marked by	*Then Subcondition Will Be Marked by*
Covenant Code (Exodus 21–23)	כי/וכי	אם/ואם
Laws of Deuteronomy (Chs. 12–26)	כי/וכי	אם/ואם
	Ø (apodictic)	כי/וכי

FIGURE 1.5. The New Method of
Constructing a Legal Unit in Deuteronomy

The redactor of the Temple Scroll must have recognized the inconsistency between the function of כי in the Covenant Code and its new role
in some Deuteronomic laws. There are four places where he incorporates
one of Deuteronomy's new legal units into the scroll, as shown in fig. 1.6.

	Tithes	*Firstlings*	*Vows*	*Witnesses*
11QT	43:12–15	52:7–12	53:11–14	61:6–12
General Rule	Deut 14:22–23	Deut 15:19–20	Deut 23:22	Deut 19:15
Casuistic Continuation	Deut 14:24–25	Deut 15:21–23	Deut 23:23	Deut 19:16–19

FIGURE 1.6. Deuteronomy's New Legal Unit in the Temple Scroll

In each of these cases, Deuteronomy's innovative use of כי to mark a
subcondition or continuation conflicted with the redactor's use of conditional כי only to mark a new law (as can be seen from the spacing system).
Retaining the Deuteronomic כי in these cases would thus have implied the
beginning of a new legal case, since this was the one normative function
for conditional כי that the redactor of the Temple Scroll recognized. But in
all of these cases, the redactor saw correctly that Deuteronomy's כי marked
only a subcondition or qualification of a main law, not the main law itself.
To resolve this inconsistency and to maintain the coherence of his system,
the redactor leveled the "anomalous" כי to אם in each case, thereby pre-
serving both the original structure of the legal unit and his own consistent
use of כי only to mark a new law.

Just as the Temple Scroll's redactor undoes Deuteronomy's voice by deleting the role of Moses as mediator, so here he undoes Deuteronomy's grammar, leveling its innovative legal syntax back to the norm represented by the Covenant Code.[77] The drive toward harmonization, toward making sense of the heterogeneity of the redacted Pentateuch goes beyond reconciling laws with conflicting content. It extends to reconciling laws with conflicting syntactical structures. In effect, the ancient redactor of the Temple Scroll was an astute historical linguist who implicitly identified and resolved the inconsistent systems of legal syntax employed by the Covenant Code, on the one hand, and Deuteronomy, on the other.

Although there are two separate triggers for the Temple Scroll's reduction of כי to אם, the redactor was actually remarkably consistent in implementing the change. When incorporating a law from Deuteronomy in which כי marked the main protasis, he sometimes retained כי unchanged or, alternatively, replaced it with אם to smooth the seams between his source texts. When the Deuteronomic law used כי to introduce the continuation of a law that began apodictically, the redactor of the Temple Scroll invariably replaced the כי with אם. The conditions for replacement can be summarized in diagram form as in fig. 1.7.

Function of כי *in Deuteronomic Source*	*Response by* 11QT
A. If it marks new law . . .	then, *either*: כי **is** retained; *or* כי is replaced by אם for redactional smoothing.
B. If it marks continuation of a preceding apodictic command or prohibition . . .	*Step 1* original definition of the legal unit is retained by placing an interval before the apodictic rule, as "new unit" marker; *Step 2* כי of source is leveled to אם.

FIGURE 1.7. The Conditions for Retention or
Replacement of Conditional כי in the Temple Scroll

77. Just as the Temple Scroll's divine voicing seems to represent a reaction against the Mosaic voice of Deuteronomy, so also the editor's situating of the text at Sinai (11QTemple 51:7; and note the reuse of Exodus 34 by 11QTemple col. 2) implicitly rejects Moab as the site of covenant-making (Deut 28:69). See Moshe Weinfeld, "God versus Moses in the Temple Scroll: 'I Do Not Speak on My Own but on God's Authority' (*Sifrei Deut.* Sec. 5; John 12,48f)," *RevQ* 15 (1991) 175–80.

The second trigger, the response to Deuteronomy's use of כי to mark a subcondition or continuation, accounts for the four remaining cases of replacement in the Temple Scroll.

Case 1: Firstlings

In his reuse of Deuteronomy's firstlings law described above, the redactor properly defined the legal unit by placing an interval before the initial apodictic statement (11QT 52:7). Since the casuistic כי that opens the exception clause stands in the middle of the unit, he reduced it to אם: ואם יהיה בו מום פסח או עור או כול מום רע, "*But if* it has a defect of lameness or blindness, or any serious defect . . ." (11QT 52:9).

Case 2: Tithes

The structure of Deuteronomy's law of tithes corresponds to the structure of the firstlings law just discussed. The unit begins with an apodictic general rule: "You shall be sure to tithe all that your seed yields: the produce of the field from year to year" (Deut 14:22). The initial formulation is followed by a subordinate clause allowing for the conversion of tithes into cash for those who live far from the temple (v. 24). The syntax of the concessive verse is difficult. It joins four consecutive כי clauses, the first three of which are conditional, the last of which is a motive clause, as in fig. 1.8.

וכי ירבה ממך הדרך	*And if* the distance is too great for you;
כי לא תוכל שאתו	*if* you are unable to carry it;
כי ירחק ממך המקום אשר יבחר	*if* the place that Yahweh has chosen . . .
יהוה אלהיך לשום שמו שם	is too distant for you,
כי יברכך יהוה אלהיך	*because* Yahweh your God has blessed you,
ונתתה בכסף . . .	you may exchange it for cash . . .

FIGURE 1.8. Proliferation of כי Clauses in Deut 14:24–25

The verse preserves several attempts to justify a legal innovation: the conversion of sancta into cash. The formulas in the first and third conditional clauses present the new law as a contingency that was anticipated from the outset, programmed into the original legal charter for life in the land.[78] The concatenation of three conditional clauses in the final form of

---

78. On the exegetical use of these formulas in Deuteronomy, see Alexander Rofé, *Introduction to Deuteronomy: Part I and Further Chapters* (2nd rev. ed.; Jerusalem: Akademon, 1988) 16 [Hebrew]; Michael Fishbane, *Biblical Interpretation in Ancient Israel* (Oxford: Clarendon, 1988) 157, 249; and Levinson, *Hermeneutics of Legal Innovation*, 39–43.

the text almost certainly represents redactional layering of originally independent attempts to justify the innovation.

For a Second-Temple exegete who was attempting to read the dia-
chronically created text synchronically, there would have been a clear need
to resolve Deuteronomy's impossibly complex syntax.[79] The redactor of
the Temple Scroll did this by extensively recasting the syntax of the law to
clarify its content.[80] In the process, he eliminated the string of כי clauses.
The initial כי protasis of the Deuteronomic law is combined with the third
conditional כי clause and reformulated as a fronted participial construction
(as in later rabbinic law). Deuteronomy's imprecise "*too distant* [ירחק] for
you" is now defined as "*at a distance* [מרחק] of three days' journey."[81] The
fourth כי clause, the motive clause, is also deleted. The one remaining
conditional כי clause, however, still presents a problem. It cannot fit the
Temple Scroll's system of regulating the use of כי. It does not represent
the beginning of a legal case, since here the case had already begun with
the apodictic rule (14:22). Accordingly, this כי also disappeared, and was
replaced with אם, as in fig. 1.9.

והיושבים במרחק מן	As for those who dwell at a distance of three
המקדש דרך שלושת ימים	days' journey from the Temple:
כול אשר יוכלו להביא	everything that they are able to bring, they may
יביאו	bring;
ואם לוא יוכלו לשאתו	*but if* they are unable to carry it,
ימכרוהו בכסף	they may sell it for cash.

FIGURE 1.9. 11QT 43:12–14

---

79. The proliferation of conditional clauses in Deut 14:24 creates difficulties even for
modern translations, which attempt to remove the redundancy by retaining only one of the
clauses, converting the second into a temporal clause, and converting the third into a relative
clause: "But if, *when* the LORD your God has blessed you, the distance is so great *that* you are
unable to transport it . . ." (NRSV). An alternative strategy is to render one as a motive clause:
"*because* the place . . . is far from you" (NJPS). The forced nature of this rendering is evident
in the fact that the NJPS had just, shortly before, correctly identified the identical clause as
conditional: "If the place . . . is too far from you" (Deut 12:21).

80. Note the replacement of the common biblical form of the infinitive construct,
without prefix (שאתו), with the form that construes it with the preposition (לשאתו). The
preposition is always affixed to the infinitive construct in Rabbinic Hebrew; the Hebrew of
the Dead Sea Scrolls reflects a strong tendency toward that form (Kutscher, *Isaiah Scroll*, 41;
and Qimron, *Hebrew of the Dead Sea Scrolls*, 47).

81. See Yadin, *Temple Scroll*, 1:315, 2:183; Emanuel Tov, "Deut. 12 and 11QTemple LII–
LIII: A Contrastative Analysis," *RevQ* 15 (1991) 169–73 (overlooking Yadin's analysis); Jeffrey
H. Tigay, *Deuteronomy: The JPS Torah Commentary* (Philadelphia: Jewish Publication Soci-
ety, 1996) 117; and Aharon Shemesh, "'Three Days' Journey from the Temple': The Use of
This Expression in the Temple Scroll," *DSD* 6 (1999) 126–38.

The recast law creates order out of Deuteronomy's disorder. The Temple Scroll's "de-editing" process is patent here. The complexity and redundancy of the Deuteronomic source text, which most likely resulted from editorial activity, are smoothed out as the redactor submits the lemma to yet another layer of editorial activity.[82]

Case 3: Witness Law

The third example begins with an apodictic statement that prohibits convicting someone on the basis of mere hearsay and, conversely, requires at least two witnesses for conviction (Deut 19:15). It is continued by a casuistic law that provides a penalty if the original law is not followed and a single witness testifies falsely against the accused. The continuation is, in effect, a legal innovation that extends talion from the realm of bodily injuries (Exod 21:24–27; Lev 24:19–20) to the realm of judicial procedures (see fig. 1.10, p. 31).[83] The structure of the unit as a whole is now:

Apodictic law (v. 15) +

Casuistic law (introduced by כי) as a continuation (vv. 16–21).

The Temple Scroll's redactor preserved this structure (11QT 61:6–12), leaving a large interval at the end of line 5 that formally marked the apodictic rule in line 6 as the beginning of the new unit. However, Deuteronomy's

---

82. A valuable test of the system proposed here would have been the Temple Scroll's reuse of Deuteronomy's concession for secular slaughter (Deut 12:20–21). As in the law of tithes (Deut 14:22–24), redactional layering, which represents successive attempts to justify innovation, results in several different types of כי clauses' being joined together:

Deut 12:20	conditional	כי ירחיב יהוה אלהיך את גבולך . . .
	motive clause	כי תאוה נפשך לאכל בשר . . .
Deut 12:21	conditional	כי ירחק ממך המקום אשר יבחר יהוה אלהיך . . .

The Temple Scroll subsequently reemployed Deut 12:20–21 in 11QT 53:07–4. Given our hypothesis that the redactor would not tolerate conditional כי in the middle of a legal unit, we would expect the second conditional clause (Deut 12:21) to somehow be removed. Since the top of col. 53 is not preserved, however, it is impossible to know how the redactor dealt with the unit (see Elisha Qimron [ed.], *The Temple Scroll: A Critical Edition with Extensive Reconstructions* [Beer-sheva: Ben-Gurion University of the Negev Press / Jerusalem: Israel Exploration Society, 1996] 77). At the same time, on linguistic grounds, the reconstruction proposed by Yadin, which coordinates two protases, each marked by כי, is unlikely (*Temple Scroll*, 2:237). When the redactor elsewhere reworks the structurally similar law of tithes (11QT 43:12–14), he rephrases it so as to remove all but one of the four כי clauses that cluster in the Deuteronomic text. In the one that remains, the original כי is replaced with אם. That the redactor took such pains not to retain multiple כי clauses within a single protasis suggests that he would have treated Deut 12:20–21 similarly.

83. See further Levinson, *Hermeneutics of Legal Innovation*, 118–23.

לא יקום עד אחד באיש לכל עון ולכל חטאת בכל חטא אשר יחטא על [15]
פי שני עדים או על פי שלשה עדים יקום דבר

כִּי יקום עד המס באיש לענות בו סרה [16]

ועמדו שני האנשים אשר להם הריב לפני יהוה לפני הכהנים והשפטים [17]
אשר יהיו בימים ההם . . .

[15] A single witness shall not prevail against a man for any wrongdoing or for any sin—in any matter in which he has sinned. On the testimony of two witnesses or on the testimony of three witnesses shall a charge be established.

[16] *If* a malicious witness comes forward against a man to testify wrongly against him,

[17] the two men who are at dispute shall go stand before Yahweh, before the priests and the judges who are officiating in those days.

FIGURE I.10. Deut 19:15–17

use of כי to continue the initial apodictic law controverted the Temple Scroll's system of restricting כי to case-defining main protases. In order to retain the structure of the unit, the redactor replaced Deuteronomy's כי with אם:

ממנו   *vacat* [5]

לוא יקום עד אחד באיש לכול עוון ולכול חטא אשר יחטא על פי שנים [6]

עדים או על פי שלושה עדים יקום דבר אִם יקום עד חמס באיש לענות [7]
הריב

בו סרה ועמדו שני האנשים אשר להמה לפני ולפני הכוהנים והלויים [8]
ולפני

[5] of him. *vacat*

[6] A single witness shall not prevail against a man for any wrongdoing or for any sin which he might commit. On the testimony of two

[7] witnesses or on the testimony of three witness shall a charge be established. *If* a malicious witness comes forward against a man, to testify

[8] falsely against him, the two men who are [at dispute] shall stand before me and before the priests and the levites and before . . .

FIGURE I.11. 11QT 61:5–8

Case 4: Vows

The final occurrence of this interchange of כי and אם appears in Deuteronomy's laws of vows (Deut 23:22–24), where the general admonition to fulfill vows is introduced by conditional כי. This form contrasts with the previous three cases. Like them, however, the opening general statement is followed by a clause formulated casuistically and marked by the use of כי. Since the redactor read the כי here as marking the continuation of the main law, this case presented the same problem for him as the preceding examples (see fig. 1.12).

כי תדר נדר ליהוה אלהיך לא תאחר לשלמו כי דרש ידרשנו יהוה אלהיך מעמך והיה בך חטא:	[22]	A [22]	If you make a vow to Yahweh your God, do not delay in fulfilling it, for Yahweh your God will surely require it of you, and it will count against you as a sin.
וכי תחדל לנדר לא יהיה בך חטא:	[23]	B [23]	But if you refrain from vowing, it will not count against you as a sin.
מוצא שפתיך תשמר ועשית כאשר נדרת ליהוה אלהיך נדבה אשר דברת בפיך: ס	[24]	A [24]	What has gone forth from your lips you must take heed to perform, just as you have vowed to Yahweh your God as a freewill offering, which you have promised by your mouth.

Figure 1.12. Deuteronomy's Laws of Vows (Deut 23:22–24)

The law's anomalous structure, with its two consecutive כי clauses, reflects a textual difficulty. The admonition to be careful to fulfill what the lips utter (v. 24), which presupposes the uttering of a vow, does not logically continue the statement that not vowing ensures freedom from culpability (v. 23). More meaningfully, it would be written so that the general homiletic rationale for fulfilling vows (v. 24) resumed the law stipulating that vows must be fulfilled (v. 22). Consequently, v. 23, which breaks the continuity between vv. 22 and 24, must be an insertion. It may have been added to the text from a different perspective, urging refraining from vows as the best course of action.[84]

---

84. See further in part 2 of this book.

This textual disturbance was sensed by various communities of readers in the Second Temple period.[85] Qoheleth, in his reception of the text (Qoh 5:3–4), updated the conditional marker to temporal כאשר, as has already been noted. More strikingly, he also reordered the law so that the encouragement not to vow no longer disrupted the continuity between the two verses concerned with fulfilling vows once they are made. Instead, it now concludes the unit in order to serve as its proper climax (see fig. 1.13).

כאשר תדר נדר לאלהים אל תאחר לשלמו [3] כי אין חפץ בכסילים את אשר תדר שלם: טוב אשר לא תדר משתדר ולא תשלם: [4]
[3]   When you make a vow to God, do not delay in fulfilling it,   for there is no delight in fools. What you vow, fulfill. [4]   Better that you should not vow than to vow and not fulfill.

FIGURE 1.13. Qoh 5:3–4

The same textual difficulty was sensed and resolved in a different way by the redactor of the Temple Scroll.[86] The insertion into the Deuteronomic text had created an impossible sequence for the redactor: a casuistic main law marked by using an initial כי was apparently continued by a subcondition that also began with כי. To resolve the difficulty, the redactor leveled the contextually disruptive second כי of the Deuteronomic lemma to אם. Moreover, the redactor accurately marked the beginning of the unit by placing an interval before the initial כי; conversely, no interval is placed before the אם (see fig. 1.14).

---

85. Postbiblical readers struggled to understand the relationship of v. 23 to the preceding verse. This struggle is reflected in a Tannaitic debate over whether it was better not to vow at all than to make and fulfill a vow (see *Sipre Deut.* §265). In the first view, v. 23 represents an independent admonition: not vowing at all, under any circumstances, guarantees that guilt will not be incurred (see also *b. Ned.* 22a, 77b). The second interpretation makes v. 23 in effect a subcondition of v. 22. The admonition that guilt would not have been incurred had no vow been made (v. 23) is thus exegetically restricted so that it refers only to cases in which a vow was made but not fulfilled (v. 22). See Lawrence H. Schiffman, "The Laws of Vows and Oaths (*Num 30,3–16*) in the Zadokite Fragments and the Temple Scroll," in *The Courtyards of the House of the Lord: Studies on the Temple Scroll* (ed. Florentino García Martínez; STDJ 75; Leiden: Brill, 2008) 557–72. See further part 2 of this book, pp. 50–53.

86. With the replacement, the redactor grammatically marks the clause as a subcondition. However, legal-exegetical concerns may have mandated that the grammatically instantiated subcondition also be read as an admonition against vowing altogether. Schiffman argues that the Temple Scroll's transformation of the syntax of Deut 23:23 has legal-exegetical significance, sharpening the verse into an admonition against making any vow at all (Schiffman, "Laws of Vows and Oaths," 207–8. See further in part 2 of this book, pp. 50–53).

וכי אם תדור נדר לוא תאחר לשלמו	[11] And if you make a vow, do not delay in fulfilling it, for I will surely require it of you,
כי דרוש אדורשנו מידכה	
והיה בכה לחטאה	[12] and it will count against you as a sin. *But if* you refrain and do not vow, it will not count against you as a sin.
ואם תחדל ולוא תדור לוא יהיה	
בכה חטאה	
מוצא שפתיכה תשמור כאשר נדרתה	[13] What your lips utter you must observe, for you have vowed freely with your mouth to do
נדבה בפיכה לעשות	
vacat כאשר נדרתה	[14] as you have vowed. *vacat*

FIGURE I.14. 11QT 53:11–14

In formal terms, the unit is now integrated into the Temple Scroll's overall consistent system for the deployment of כי, and it is clearly demarcated as a legal-literary unit. The redactor was actually less "invasive" in correcting the textual disturbance of the MT than was the author of Qoheleth, whose surgery was far more substantial.

VII. Pleonastic Marking of the Protasis

In two instances in the Temple Scroll, neither אם nor כי introduces the protasis. Rather, the two clauses are joined asyndetically, so that the protasis is redundantly marked by a double conditional. The occurrence of this pleonasm provides us with an opportunity to test the model proposed here in which an ostensibly syntactical issue is best explained in terms of a redactor's engagement with the biblical text (fig. I.15).

11QT 53:11	וכי אם תדר נדר לוא תאחר לששלמו . . .
	And if₁ if₂ you make a vow, do not delay in fulfilling it . . .
11QT 58:10	וכי אם תחזק המלחמה עליו . . .
	And if₁ if₂ the battle becomes too strong for him . . .

FIGURE I.15. The Two Cases of the Pleonasm in the Temple Scroll

The specific form וכי אם rules out two alternative interpretations that would avoid the redundancy.[87] The form with the copula cannot represent

---

87. Thus, any analogy to certain cases where כי אם, after a negative, introduces an adversative clause (Gen 32:39) is similarly ruled out, or where כי אם introduces an affirmative

the standard formula for an exception clause in Biblical Hebrew, כִּי אִם,
"but rather."[88] Neither in Biblical Hebrew nor in the Temple Scroll does
the exception clause ever appear with initial *waw*.[89] Nor is it feasible that
each particle functions independently, to mean, in effect, "and because,
if. . . ." Figure 1.16 represents all occurrences of וכי in the Temple Scroll
(the digraph וכיא does not appear). There is no case in the Temple Scroll
where וכי introduces a motive clause, to mean "and because."[90] Instead,
without exception, every attestation of וכי in the scroll marks a legal protasis and means "and if."

Form	11QT	Source	Meaning in Source
וכי אם	53:11	כי (Deut 23:22a) (Syriac assumes וכי)	If
וכי אם	58:10	— *<no clear biblical precedent>*	
וכי	60:12	וכי (Deut 18:6)	And if
וכי	61:2	וכי (Deut 18:21)	And if

FIGURE 1.16. וכי in the Temple Scroll

Accordingly, the only way to read the Temple Scroll's anomalous וכי
אם is as a pleonasm. The syntagm is, in effect, a redactor's uncorrected
"stutter," with the two alternative conditionals redundantly marking a
single protasis: "if if."

The two cases of the pleonasm warrant further attention. Brin has
offered several mutually exclusive interpretations. The most convincing
suggestion is that the doubling reflects the interference between the redactor's "living" language (which knew only אם as the standard conditional)

---

oath (2 Kgs 5:20; Jer 51:14). In such cases, the אם is sometimes regarded as "pleonastic"; see
Ronald J. Williams, *Hebrew Syntax: An Outline* (revised and expanded by John C. Beckman;
3rd ed.; Toronto: University of Toronto Press, 2007) §§447, 457; Schoors, "Particle כי," 250,
252. In none of these cases is a conditional use at issue; nor is there ever an initial copula.

88. On this use in Biblical Hebrew to mark exception or adversative clauses, see ibid.,
251–53.

89. The Temple Scroll uses כי אם as an exception clause in 3:6; 48:12; 52:14; and 57:16.
There are 120 attestations in the Hebrew Bible, e.g., Gen 32:29; Exod 12:9; Lev 21:14; Deut
12:14; 16:6; see Even-Shoshan, *New Concordance of the Old Testament*, 532–33.

90. Failure to note the *waw* results in the impossible translation "for if" in 11QTemple
53:11, as in Johann Maier, *The Temple Scroll: An Introduction, Translation, and Commentary*
(JSOTSup 34; Sheffield: JSOT Press, 1985) 47. In the Temple Scroll, וכי is never causative.
Aside from the grammatical difficulty, it is also unclear how introducing the law on vows
with a causative, "*for* if you make a vow," could make any contextual sense. Note that Maier
translates וכי אם simply "and if" in 11QTemple 58:10, the other occurrence of the pleonasm.

and his attempts to reproduce biblical syntax.[91] This solution regards the pleonasm as essentially random. It can provide no specific reason for the pleonasms' occurring only where they did and not in other places in the scroll.[92] However, the pleonasms should not be regarded simply in terms of grammatical or linguistic confusion. At issue here is much more the redactor's confrontation with a multiplicity of biblical sources, resulting in the attempt to straddle competing literary models. The redundancy can only be satisfactorily understood by examining the redactor's stance as a hermeneute who revised and re-edited his sources.

Case 1: The Pleonasm in the Law of Vows

The first instance of pleonasm appeared as the redactor made the transition from laws of sacrifice to laws of vows. Seeking to construct a comprehensive section about vows (11QT 53:9–54:7), he combined material from three different textual sources. Immediately preceding the section on vows, the Temple Scroll contains a reworked version of Deuteronomy's law permitting secular slaughter while restricting all sacrificial slaughter to the

---

91. Brin, "Bible in Temple Scroll," 217. In the same article, Brin provides an alternative explanation of the pleonasm in terms of the concept of a "double reading" (ibid., 215 and n. 7). Since in none of these cases is there manuscript or versional evidence that suggests a "reading" with אם alone, there is no real basis for explaining the text as a "double reading." Properly speaking, a "double reading" implies that a copyist has combined two separate manuscript variants side by side, without attempting to choose between them. See Robert Gordis, *The Biblical Text in the Making: A Study of the Kethib-Qere* (Hoboken, N.J.: Ktav, 1971); and, most systematically, Shemaryahu Talmon, "Double Readings in the Massoretic Text," *Text and Canon of the Hebrew Bible: Collected Studies* (Winona Lake, IN: Eisenbrauns, 2010) 217–66; and idem, "Synonymous Readings in the Masoretic Text," in ibid., 171–216. Note Tov's cautions (*Textual Criticism*, 163–65, 225–27, 257–58).

Brin has recently offered a third explanation of the pleonasms. Because conditional כי was no longer familiar when the Temple Scroll was composed, the redactor glossed it with אם to clarify its conditional function (idem, "Divorce at Qumran," in *Legal Texts and Legal Issues* [ed. Moshe J. Bernstein, Florentino García Martínez, and John Kampen; STDJ 23; Leiden: Brill, 1997] 231–44 [at pp. 237–38]). This argument encounters a significant difficulty: in one of the two cases of the pleonasm (11QTemple 58:10), there was no biblical Vorlage with כי that needed to be clarified. Similarly untenable is the analogy drawn by Brin in the same article between the pleonasm in the Temple Scroll (וכי אם) and the formulation כי אם in 4QMinor Prophets[a] Mal 2:16. The analysis overlooks the significance of the copulative *waw* present in the pleonasms in the Temple Scroll but absent in 4QXII[a]: the copula specifies that the formula functions as a conditional (see fig. 1.16). Furthermore, there is clear evidence in 4QXII[a] that each conjunction retains its independent force, so that the formulation means "but if." The scroll thus transforms the condemnation of divorce by the MT into permission. See the perceptive analysis of Russell Fuller, "Text-Critical Problems in Malachi 2:10–16," *JBL* 110 (1991) 45–57 (at pp. 55–57).

92. Similarly vague is explaining the pleonasm as "die Verlegenheit des Authors (des Kopisten?) gegenüber den grammatischen Problemen . . . , mit denen er konfrontiert war" (Thorion, "Sprache der Tempelrolle," 426).

central sanctuary (Deut 12:20–25). The missing top of col. 53 makes it unclear whether the double Deuteronomic protasis with כי was preserved in
the Temple Scroll.[93] In moving to the new topic, the redactor transformed
the appendix in Deuteronomy's laws of sacrifice. The latter included a
metonymic reference to נדריך "your votive [offerings]" as being one of the
sacrifices that, henceforth, must be offered at the central sanctuary alone
(Deut 12:26). That appendix was reworked so that it now introduced the
unit on vows. The transition between the two units was effected by means
of word association, because the key term of the Deuteronomic law of
"vows" is, in the singular, the similar-looking word נדר (Deut 23:22–24).
This law uses כי twice to mark the protasis. Finally, consistent with his program of joining material on similar topics, the redactor also incorporated
the Priestly legislation on vows (Num 30:3–16). These laws begin with the
common Priestly formula of *casus pendens* with a relative clause (איש/אשה
כי; 11QT 53:14, 16 = Num 30:3, 4). Then, however, they shift to numer-
ous subconditions formulated with ואם (11QT 53:19–54:1 = Num 30:6–16).
Following the unit on vows, the redactor moved to the long series of
apostasy laws (grouping Deut 13:2–19 and 17:2–5). Here, the MT כי (Deut
13:2, 7, 13; 17:2) was recast as (ו)אם (11QT 54:8, 19; 55:2, 15; see fig. 1.17).

Biblical Source	Protasis Marker	11QTemple	Protasis Marker	Topic
Deut 12:20–25	כי	53:07–8	[?]	Laws of sacrifice
12:26	Ø (appendix)	53:9–10	Ø (introduction)	**Laws about vowing**
Deut 23:22–24	כי וכי	53:11–13	וכי אם אם	
Num 30:3–5	איש/אשה כי	53:14–19	איש / אשה כי	
Num 30:6–16	ואם	53:19–54:7	ואם	
Deut 13:2–19 + 17:2–5	כי	54:8–56:11	אם	Laws of apostasy

FIGURE 1.17. The Redactional Context
of the Pleonastic Conditionals (11QTemple 53:11)

93. See n. 82 above.

The context of the pleonasm in 53:11 is thus a complex literary transition that splices together three separate legal topoi and three different forms of legal syntax. The double particle indicates that the redactor was already thinking ahead to the new sections. It resulted from the interference between his source text (כי תדר נדר; Deut 23:22) and the long series of subconditions beginning with אם that he anticipated would follow. He held both forms of the conditional in his mind simultaneously, as the replacement of MT וכי (Deut 23:23) with אם in the very next line confirms (11QT 53:12). In the midst of a multilayered transition, keeping the two conditionals straight proved too difficult, and the redactor accidentally deployed them both at the point of overlap.

Case 2: The Pleonasm in the Law of the King

The second pleonasm appears in the Temple Scroll's Law of the King (cols. 57–59). Part of this unit, col. 58, is formulated as a sequence of increasing military threats against the monarch that are met with corresponding responses. By emphasizing the king's active role, the redactor restored to the monarch the traditional military leadership that was denied him in the war laws in Deuteronomy, which passed by without mentioning him (see fig. 1.18)

11QT	Condition (Protasis)	Military Situation	Monarch's Response (Apodosis)
58:3	A. והיה כי	Enemy Threat: Case 1	¹⁄₁₀ of the people are sent
58:6	B. ואם	Case 2	⅕ are sent
58:7	C. ואם	Case 3	⅓ are sent
58:10	D. וכי אם	Case 4	½ are sent
58:11	E. והיה אם	Israelite Defeat of Enemy	all of the people divide the spoils
58:15	א F. ו[ע]ם	Offensive Warfare (כי תצא למלחמה; Deut 20:1)	⅕ of the people are sent

FIGURE 1.18. Military Situation and Incremental Royal Response: The Context for the Pleonasm in 11QT 58:10

The redactor here followed a consistent structural plan: all cases after the initial case (והיה כי) were marked as subordinate by the use of אם. This

consistency is especially evident in the replacement of כי with אם in 11QT
58:15, which is modeled on the Deuteronomic protasis כי תצא למלחמה
(Deut 20:1). The conditional form in the new section on victory, והיה אם
(11QT 58:11), parallels the opening והיה כי (58:3). On analogy with the subordinate status of והיה אם in Deuteronomic law (Deut 20:11; 21:14; 25:2),
11QT 58:11 'most likely represented the beginning of a new subtopic—the
case of an Israelite victory—that was still a part of the same larger unit, the
laws of royal war.

Against the backdrop of this formal structure, conflicting literary
precedents gave rise to the pleonasm וכי אם. The text was formulated as a
conditional statement applying to a situation in which the king required
reinforcements:

וכי אם תחזק המלחמה עליו ושלחו לו מחצית העם

And if₁ if₂ the battle intensifies against him, then they shall send
him half the people. (11QTemple 58:10)

There is only one case in the Bible where, as here, the verb חזק is construed
with המלחמה as its subject.[94] This verse, 2 Kgs 3:26, describes a situation
parallel to the situation that our author is trying to describe: a monarch
facing overwhelming odds in a battle that is turning against him. It also
contains the essential formal elements: כי (although as relative rather than
conditional) מלחמה + חזק + (as subject):

וירא מלך מואב כי חזק ממנו המלחמה

The king of Moab saw *that the battle had become too severe* for him.
(2 Kgs 3:26)

Here, however, the key verb, חזק, appears in the perfect. Following the
convention of Classical Semitic languages, the verb precedes the subject, and the verb is masculine despite the fact that its subject, מלחמה, is
grammatically feminine.[95] An alternate literary model provides the third-
person-feminine imperfect form (תחזק) that appears in 11QTemple 58:10.
The topic also matches that of the Temple Scroll: the overwhelming esca-
lation of a battle.

---

94. Otherwise "battle" is the direct or indirect object of the verb. It may refer either to
intensifying the battle (2 Sam 11:25; 2 Chr 25:8) or to mustering one's courage in preparation
for battle (Josh 11:20).

95. See Bruce K. Waltke and Michael O'Connor, *Introduction to Biblical Hebrew Syntax* (Winona Lake, IN: Eisenbrauns, 1990) 109. Second Temple Hebrew generally followed
the later convention of consistent gender agreement.

ויאמר אם תחזק ארם ממני . . .

He said, "*If* the Arameans *are too strong* for me. . . ."
(2 Sam 10:11 = 1 Chr 19:12)

Here, however, it is אם that is employed as the dependent clause marker:
אם תחזק. Thus, both this model and 2 Kgs 3:26 contain either כי or אם
plus the root חזק in the context of battle. The interference between the
two produced the pleonasm that asyndetically joined both forms of the
conditional (fig. 1.19).

A. 2 Kgs 3:26	כי + חזק + <u>המלחמה</u>
+ B. 2 Sam 10:11; 1 Chr 19:2	<u>אם</u> + תחזק
= C. 11QTemple 58:10	וכי אם תחזק המלחמה

FIGURE 1.19. The Literary Sources for the Pleonasm in 11QT 58:10

Besides this conflict between direct textual sources, the redundancy
was made almost inevitable by the competition between the two separate
literary models that governed the column as a whole. On the one hand,
the protases for Deuteronomy's war laws (one of the starting points for
the unit) employ כי (Deut 20:1, 10). On the other hand, the literary structure of the column required each of the series of incremental conditions
to begin consistently with אם(ו), as line 11 and, especially, the correction
in line 15 confirm.

VIII. The Broader Significance
of the Pleonasms

The factors that gave rise to the two inadvertent pleonasms in the
Temple Scroll may have a precedent in one case in the legal corpora
of the Pentateuch. Here also, in the wake of a redactor's working with
competing literary models for marking a dependent clause, as a law was
"translated" from the legal syntax of one source into that of another source,
it seems inadvertently to have received a double conditional.[96] Isolated
though this case is, it opens up a larger perspective for understanding

---

96. The Covenant Code's prohibition on cursing parents is expanded into a chiastic
homily by the redactor of the Holiness Code. In the process, the law's protasis is redrafted
from participial into conditional formulation:

the Temple Scroll. In his re-redaction, re-systemization, and expansion of pentateuchal law, the redactor of the Temple Scroll continued the kind of editorial work that first gave rise to the Covenant Code, the legal corpus of Deuteronomy, and the Holiness Code, and that, in a final flourishing, led to the anthologizing of the three legal collections along with their accompanying narratives into the Pentateuch. Seen from this perspective, the Temple Scroll's redactor becomes the mature apprentice trained in the workshop of the Pentateuch redactor. To be sure, the goals were different. The redactor of the Pentateuch sought to preserve differences: to maintain the separate identities of his legal-literary sources, despite their separate lexicon and their inconsistent laws. The hermeneutics of the Temple Scroll point in the opposite direction: they seek to lessen the redundancies and contradictions that resulted from the conservative editing of the Pentateuch. Nonetheless, in responding to, reacting against, and rearranging the canonical Pentateuch, the redactor of the Temple Scroll continued his predecessor's magisterial accomplishment.

ומקלל אביו ואמו מות יומת	He who *curses his father or his mother shall be put to death.* (Exod 21:17)
כי איש איש אשר יקלל את אביו ואת אמו מות יומת אביו ואמו קלל דמיו בו	If [if] anyone *curses his father or his mother, he shall be put to death*: His father and his mother has he cursed—his blood is upon him. (Lev 20:9)

FIGURE 1.20. The Redrafting of the Covenant Code's Law against Cursing Parents in the Holiness Code

In the process of being redrafted, the law's protasis was given a double conditional. The formulation כי איש איש אשר (Lev 20:9) combines two separate protasis markers that are elsewhere always kept distinct: (1) conditional כי in initial position, which would normally continue with a verb in the imperfect; and (2) the Priestly *casus pendens*, comprising (a) a double subject (איש איש) in initial position (often with the partitive מבית ישראל) + (b) a relative clause introduced by אשר (see Lev 17:3, 8, 10, 13; 20:2; 22:18).

The first to establish this redundancy was Simeon Chavel, "At the Boundary of Textual and Literary Criticisms: The Case of כי in Lev 20:9," *Textus* 20 (2000) 61–70. He correctly notes that the formulation is a hapax in biblical law (see also Ezek 14:7, which involves the causal use of כי). His explaining the redundancy away as simply a later copyist's error, however, overlooks the implications of his own analysis. The double marking more likely arose at the time of the composition and redaction of the text. It seems to represent the literary "static" or interference created by the competition between rival models for the drafting of casuistic legal statements in the Holiness Code. See Meir Paran, who astutely demonstrates the redrafting of Exod 21:17 in Lev 20:9, in *Forms of the Priestly Style in the Pentateuch: Patterns, Linguistic Usages, Syntactic Structures* (Jerusalem: Magnes, 1989) 39–40 [Hebrew]. On the different forms of casuistic law in the Holiness Code, see (among a vast number of sources) Henning Graf Reventlow, *Das Heiligkeitsgesetz: Formgeschichtlich untersucht* (WMANT 6; Neukirchen-Vluyn: Neukirchener Verlag, 1961) 36–40.

IX. Conclusion

Understanding the Temple Scroll's use of language requires understanding the redactor's hermeneutics. In his reuse of the legal material of the Pentateuch, the Temple Scroll's redactor inevitably needed to confront and resolve the Pentateuch's lack of a unified system—not just in the arrangement and content of its laws but also in their formulation. The redactor's historical distance from the biblical text only intensified the difficulty of understanding its diverse systems of law and syntax on their own terms, let alone the complex literary and redactional history that brought them together. Later rabbinic law sought to harmonize the Pentateuch's legal inconsistencies and redundancies by means of exegesis. In the case of the Temple Scroll, the corresponding drive to ameliorate the Pentateuch's "disorder" took place on the level of the text by means of reordering and expanding. The commitment to Torah therefore required reordering the Torah. The same commitment gave the redactor the mandate to develop a coherent system for deploying the conditionals that distinguish the casuistic laws of the Torah.

The unification of linguistics and hermeneutics proposed here has methodological implications. The previous impasse in solving the problem of the conditionals reflects a corresponding impasse at the disciplinary level. When the problem is addressed only within the realm of linguistics, the spacing system of the manuscript, which presupposes an attempt to structure the text based on its content, is not considered relevant. When historical linguistics takes the history of interpretation into account, however, the spacing system provides essential evidence for establishing the logic behind the replacements. Conversely, hermeneutics requires historical linguistics. Were it not for the particular linguistic complexities raised by כי, there would be no reason for such a highly regulated correlation between the use of the conditional and the scroll's spacing system.

The Temple Scroll's use of conditionals therefore demonstrates the redactor's sophistication as a reader of his sources and his accomplishment as an editor. His engagement with the biblical text in the service of improving it was not limited to large-scale rearrangements of law or changes in voicing. His engagement with the biblical text permeated the scroll to its very language and syntax. In presenting what purported to be direct discourse from God, the redactor made regular inroads into the text to systematize its order and syntax, to rearrange its sequence, and to re-voice or to "de-voice" texts that were originally attributed to Moses. Paradoxically, the rejection of all mediation, whether Mosaic or editorial, could only be accomplished by increasing the degree of human mediation of that revelation. Precisely in the archaizing attempt to deny literary history, the author disclosed the fact that his work was not "original" but hermeneutical and redactional. The Temple Scroll was the creation of a community engaged with a scriptural tradition and a scriptural language from which they were long distant and yet whose pristine, revelatory voice they sought, "hand in hand, with wandering steps and slow," to revivify and claim as their own.[97]

---

97. John Milton, *Paradise Lost* (ed. Alastair Fowler; London: Longman, 1971) 642 (12.648).

PART 2

Reception History as a Window into Composition History: Deuteronomy's Law of Vows

התר נדרים פורחים באויר ואין להם על מה שיסמכו

[The rules about] release from vows hover in the air and have naught to support them.

—*m. Ḥagigah* 1:8[1]

---

1. My translation slightly modifies Herbert Danby, *The Mishnah* (London: Oxford University Press and Cumberledge, 1933) 211–16 (at p. 212).

I. Introduction: Does the Sequence of Deuteronomy's Law of Vows Logically Cohere?

Deuteronomy's law of vows (Deut 23:22–24 [LXX 23:21–23]) consists of a general admonition to fulfill vows:[2]

A [22]	כי תדר נדר ליהוה אלהיך לא תאחר לשלמו כי דרש ידרשנו יהוה אלהיך מעמך והיה בך חטא
B [23]	וכי תחדל לנדר לא יהיה בך חטא
C [24]	מוצא שפתיך תשמר ועשית כאשר נדרת ליהוה אלהיך נדבה אשר דברת בפיך

A [22] If you make a vow to Yahweh your God, you must not delay in fulfilling it, for Yahweh your God will surely require it of you, and it will count against you as a sin.

B [23] But if you refrain from vowing, it will not count against you as a sin.

C [24] What has gone forth from your lips you must take heed to perform, just as you have vowed to Yahweh your God as a freewill offering, which you have promised by your mouth.

FIGURE 2.1. Deuteronomy's Law of Vows (Deut 23:22–24)

The component parts of the unit can be designated and summarized as follows:

v. 22: **A**   If you vow, pay promptly; otherwise, it is sin.
v. 23: **B**   If you do not vow, no sin.
v. 24: **C**   Be sure to pay promptly what you vow.

A surface reading of the law reveals that its sequence is curious to the point of being problematic. The concession identified as B (v. 23) וכי תחדל לנדר לא יהיה בך חטא ("But if you refrain from vowing, it will not count against you as a sin") represents the antithesis of the previous verse, A (v. 22), following it nearly verbatim except for the negation. The problem emerges

_____
2. All translations are mine unless otherwise noted.

47

once the reader gets to C (v. 24), which urges the addressee to be careful to fulfill what the lips utter. This admonition is a non sequitur: it is difficult to see how it follows B logically (v. 23), since it presupposes the uttering of a vow (A, v. 22). One may well imagine a legal draftsman wanting to provide a moral alternative, to discourage vowing as a risky behavior, but if clarity and intelligibility were of much importance, the statement in B would make more sense at the end of the unit so as not to break up the connection between A and C.

The law of vows is located in a section that focuses on the ethical and moral obligations of the covenant community (Deut 23:16–25:19). Following the prohibition on returning escaped slaves (23:16–17) and the restrictions on exploiting prostitutes (23:18–19), Deuteronomy restricts the economic exploitation of fellow Israelites (23:20–21).[3] It is in this context that the law of vows is embedded. Historical-critical scholars have established the literary context of the law of vows and the nature of the legal corpus (Deuteronomy 12–26) in which the law appears, but they have not recognized a problem with the law's sequence.[4] Nor have major studies of vows and oaths in the Hebrew Bible taken note of the disorder in the law of vows.[5]

---

3. Bernard M. Levinson, "Deuteronomy," in *The Jewish Study Bible* (Oxford: Oxford University Press, 2004) 414, 419–20.

4. See Carl Steuernagel, *Übersetzung und Erklärung der Bücher Deuteronomium und Josua und allgemeine Einleitung in den Hexateuch* (HKAT; Göttingen: Vandenhoeck & Ruprecht, 1900) 87; idem, *Das Deuteronomium übersezt und erklärt* (2nd ed.; Göttingen Handkommentar zum Alten Testament; Göttingen: Vandenhoeck & Ruprecht, 1923) 137–38; Samuel Rolles Driver, *A Critical and Exegetical Commentary on Deuteronomy* (3rd ed.; ICC; Edinburgh: T. & T. Clark, 1902) 267–68; Alfred Bertholet, *Deuteronomium* (KHC 5; Leipzig: Mohr, 1899) 74; George Adam Smith, *The Book of Deuteronomy: In the Revised Version with Introduction and Notes* (Cambridge Bible for Schools and Colleges; Cambridge: Cambridge University Press, 1918) 275; and Gustav Hölscher, "Komposition und Ursprung des Deuteronomiums," *ZAW* 40 (1922) 161–255 (esp. p. 214 n. 1).

5. See Jacques Berlinerblau, *The Vow and the "Popular Religious Groups" of Ancient Israel: A Philological and Sociological Inquiry* (JSOTSup 210; Sheffield: Sheffield Academic Press, 1996); and Tony W. Cartledge, *Vows in the Hebrew Bible and the Ancient Near East* (JSOTSup 147; Sheffield: Sheffield Academic Press, 1992). Two other studies are less relevant for the purposes here. Hubert Tita's study is primarily synchronic and theological and does not take into account biblical law (*Gelübde als Bekenntnis: Eine Studie zu den Gelübden im Alten Testament* [OBO 181; Freiburg Schweiz: Universitätsverlag / Göttingen: Vandenhoeck & Ruprecht, 2001]). Blane Conklin's recent study maintains that there is a single rule for the syntax of legal material in "Exodus, Leviticus, and Deuteronomy" (*Oath Formulas in Biblical Hebrew* [Linguistic Studies in Ancient West Semitic 5; Winona Lake, IN: Eisenbrauns, 2011] 46). Conklin's canonical generalizations do not take into account the scholarly literature that demonstrates that different rules operate in the Covenant Code, the legal corpus of Deuteronomy, and the Holiness Code. Conklin overlooks, for example, Bernard M. Levinson and Molly M. Zahn, "Revelation Regained: The Hermeneutics of כי and אם in

Even though it has not been explicitly recognized, the disrupted sequence of the law of vows has created problems for modern translators, who have struggled to translate the passage and found it necessary to resort to implicit text criticism in order to make the sequence of thought comprehensible. For example, the NJPS translation inverts the protasis and the apodosis of Deut 23:23 in order to smooth the transition from v. 22 to v. 23. In v. 22, the focus is on the penalty for not fulfilling a vow, whereas in v. 23 the focus becomes the nonpenalty for not doing a religious act that is voluntary in the first place:[6]

[22] **כי** תדר נדר ליהוה אלהיך לא תאחר לשלמו כי דרש ידרשנו יהוה
אלהיך מעמך והיה בך חטא

[23] **וכי** תחדל לנדר לא יהיה בך חטא

[22]   **When** you make a vow to the LORD your God, do not
put off fulfilling it, for the LORD your God will require it
of you, and you will have incurred guilt;

[23]   whereas you incur no guilt **if** you refrain from vowing.

Along with the inversion of the protasis and apodosis in v. 23, the NJPS translates the word **וכי** "whereas . . . if," which is a meaning that is unattested in the legal corpus of Deuteronomy. These changes simply underscore the difficulty of reading the law of vows on its own terms.

Karl Marti offers a paraphrase that alters the law's sequence in his implicit response to the law's lack of coherence. In his summary of the law of vows, Marti is forced to rearrange the sequence of the provisions in order to make it logically coherent: "Wer kein Gelübde tut, sündigt nicht; wer aber ein Gelübde tut, muß es auch pünktlich halten [He who vows not, sins not; however, he who vows must promptly fulfill it]."[7] Recall that we can designate the different component parts of the unit this way:

v. 22: A   If you vow, pay promptly; otherwise, it is a sin
v. 23: B   If you do not vow, no sin
v. 24: C   Be sure to pay promptly what you vow

---

the Temple Scroll," *DSD* 9 (2002) 295–346; and Udo Rüterswörden ("Die Apodosis in den Rechtssätzen des Deuteronomiums," *ZAH* 15/16 [2002–3] 124–37).

6. *Tanakh: The Holy Scriptures: The New JPS Translation according to the Traditional Hebrew Text* (Philadelphia: Jewish Publication Society, 1988) 311.

7. Karl Marti, "Das fünfte Buch Mose oder Deuteronomium," in *Die Heilige Schrift des Alten Testaments* (ed. Alfred Bertholet and Emil Kautzsch; 2 vols.; 4th ed.; Tübingen: J. C. B. Mohr [Paul Siebeck], 1922–23) 1:258–327 (at p. 303).

As the following diagram shows, Marti's paraphrase establishes the logical "join" between A and C by removing the "intrusive" B, which he shifts to the beginning:

v. 23: B   If you do not vow, no sin
v. 22: A   If you vow, pay promptly; otherwise, it is a sin
v. 24: C   Be sure to pay promptly what you vow

The inversion by the NJPS and in Marti's paraphrase reflect the attempt by modern scholars to smooth out the same difficulties in the law of vows as were encountered by a number of Second Temple authors—especially those who patterned new legal or ethical compositions on pentateuchal models. They, too, struggled to make sense of the problematic sequence.

As has become increasingly recognized, the historical-critical method that characterizes academic biblical studies too often remains separate from approaches stressing the history of interpretation, which are employed most frequently in the areas of Second Temple or Dead Sea Scrolls research.[8] I argue that a review of the history of interpretation shows that readers—both ancient and modern—have attempted to rearrange the law's sequence or to rework its legal syntax. These attempts to work around or smooth over the difficulty are indicative of v. 23's being an interpolation. The interpolation can be explained in terms of wider Second Temple reservations about the wisdom of vowing. In this way, reception history provides a window onto composition history.

II. Early Jewish and Christian Reception of Deuteronomy's Law of Vows and Concerns about the Wisdom of Vowing

In part I, we saw how the Temple Scroll struggled with the difficult syntax and sequence of Deuteronomy's law of vows.[9] The author of the Temple Scroll was constrained by his own laws governing the use of כי to posit v. 23, in effect, as a subcondition. Reading the verse as a subcondition would suggest an exegetical restriction, whereas the verse refers only

---

8. See Reinhard G. Kratz, "Der Pescher Nahum und seine biblische Vorlage," *Prophetenstudien: Kleine Schriften II* (FAT 74; Tübingen: Mohr Siebeck, 2011) 99–145. Kratz's essay marks a methodological advance. Building on his previous work, Kratz fully integrates historical-critical and history of interpretation approaches. He begins with an analysis of pesher Nahum, 4QpNah (4Q169), systematically examines its reinterpretation of the biblical book of Nahum, and then works back to analyze the formation of the biblical book. In the concluding section, "Vom Orakel zum Pescher," Kratz demonstrates the relevance of the history of interpretation for conventional questions of composition and redaction.

9. See part I of this book, pp. 32–34.

to cases in which vows have already been made. In this case, the Temple Scroll author read the law similarly to R. Judah, who was engaged in a later Tannaitic debate over whether it was better not to vow at all than to make and fulfill a vow (see *Sipre Deut.* §265).[10] According to R. Judah, v. 23 is in effect a subcondition of v. 22. The admonition that guilt would not have been incurred had no vow been made (v. 23) is thus exegetically restricted so that it refers only to the cases in which a vow was made but not fulfilled (v. 22), rather than as an independent admonition not to vow at all. However, a problem emerges here. The Temple Scroll's system of legal syntax is in tension with its halakic interests. The leveling of כי to אם, which, according to the scroll's own syntactical rules, effectively renders the verse a subcondition, conflicts with the scroll's general rejection of vowing as legitimate. The author of the scroll syntactically reworks Deuteronomy's וכי תחדל לנדר ("But if you refrain from vowing") to ואם תחדל ולוא תדור ("But if you refrain and do not vow"). After changing כי to אם, the author proceeds to effectively sharpen v. 23 into an independent admonition against making any vow at all. As Lawrence H. Schiffman maintains: "Although the use of *'im* for MT *ki* is a linguistic feature of the *Temple Scroll*, the change to *we-lo' tiddor* cannot be explained except as a halakhic variation."[11] With the change from לנדר to ולוא תדור, the author of the Temple Scroll transforms the text in a way that resembles the later view of R. Meir, who was R. Judah's Tannaitic opponent. According to R. Meir, v. 23 represents an independent admonition: not vowing at all, under any circumstances, guarantees that guilt will not be incurred (see also *b. Ned.* 22a, 77b). On the one hand, the leveling of the ambiguous וכי to ואם was mandated by the Temple Scroll's internal syntactical law governing the use of כי and אם. On the other hand, the attempt to sharpen the negation in the name of its legal exegetical concerns points to wider Second Temple concerns regarding the wisdom of vowing. In its struggle to articulate and hold together its own conflicting agendas (syntactic and halakic), both of which center on v. 23, the Temple Scroll is a prime example of the way in which a study of the reception history can reveal a problem with the received text—a problem that is in this particular case, as we shall see, attributable to an interpolation.

Like the Temple Scroll, the Septuagint is evidence of a trend in which Second Temple scribes struggled with the issue of vows and oaths and

---

10. On the *Sipre*, see also pp. 61–65 of part 2.

11. See Lawrence H. Schiffman, "The Laws of Vows and Oaths (*Num 30, 3–16*) in the Zadokite Fragments and the Temple Scroll," *RevQ* 15 (1991) 199–214 (at pp. 207–8). Although unnoticed by Schiffman, this position was anticipated already by Yigael Yadin, *The Temple Scroll* (3 vols.; Jerusalem: Israel Exploration Society, 1977–83) 2:239.

with the troublesome v. 23 of Deuteronomy's law of vows, specifically.[12] The Septuagint differs from the MT in two respects relevant to the analysis here: (1) Whereas MT Deut 23:22 reads כי, the corresponding Septuagint assumes וכי, reading δέ (LXX Deut 23:21), as in Deut 15:16.[13] (2) The Hebrew verb in the protasis of v. 23, וכי תחדל, should be translated "But if you *refrain* from vowing. . . ."[14] The Septuagint translator renders, instead: θέλῃς, "But if you do not *wish* to vow." This is the only time θέλῃς is used to translate חדל in the Septuagint.[15] In effect, vowing and not vowing are not being treated here as mere alternatives that are equivalent, as appears to be the case in the MT: "The point which the translator is making is that there is no compelling reason for making a vow in the first place; a vow is only made if one wishes to do so, and only if one has made this voluntary promise is there an obligation to carry it out."[16]

Lawrence Schiffman argues that in the *Damascus Document* all binding oaths must either be fulfilled if commanded by the Torah or annulled if the oath would in some way violate the Torah.[17] The author of the *Damascus Document* cites only the first clause of v. 24 of Deuteronomy's law on vows (מוצא שפתיך תשמר ועשית, "What has gone forth from your lips you

---

12. The hypothesis that v. 23 represents an interpolation does not find clear support in the versions. The verse itself is witnessed in all of the major textual traditions, including the LXX, Syr., Vg., and the Aramaic tgs. (where the Palestinian traditions, as expected, add exegetical expansions). The three Deuteronomy MSS extant at Qumran that preserve portions of the law of vows (4QDeut^f, 4QDeut^i, 4QDeut^k2 [= 4Q33, 4Q36, 4Q38a]), though very fragmentary, suggest that no significant textual variations are present. See Eugene Ulrich et al., eds., *Qumran Cave 4.IX: Deuteronomy to Kings* (DJD 14; Oxford: Clarendon, 1995) 52, 74, 102. Coeditor Sidnie White Crawford deals with 4QDeut^f and 4QDeut^i, while coeditor Julie Ann Duncan deals with 4QDeut^k2.The initial part of the protasis of v. 23, וכי תחדל, is preserved in 4QDeut^i (with the *waw* and *kap* only partially preserved).

13. John William Wevers, *Notes on the Greek Text of Deuteronomy* (SBLSCS 39; Atlanta: Scholars Press, 1995) 374.

14. The meaning that *TDOT* provides for חדל in Deut 23:23 essentially matches the third definition provided by *HALOT* 1:292 ("to refrain").

15. Edwin Hatch and Henry A. Redpath, *A Concordance to the Septuagint and the Other Greek Versions of the Old Testament [Including the Apocryphal Books]* (repr., 2 vols. in 1; Grand Rapids, MI: Baker, 1998) 1:628–29. See also Wevers, *Notes on the Greek Text*, 374. For the wide variety of Greek words used in the Septuagint to translate other occurrences of חדל, see Takamitsu Muraoka, *Hebrew/Aramaic Index to the Septuagint: Keyed to the Hatch-Redpath Concordance* (Grand Rapids, MI: Baker, 1998) 47. For the meaning of θέλῃς, although the passage from the law of vows is not cited, see Takamitsu Muraoka, *A Greek-English Lexicon of the Septuagint* (Leuven: Peeters, 2009) 326.

16. Wevers, *Notes on the Greek Text*, 374. Although he does not deal directly with the conditionals of Deuteronomy's law of vows, for a recent study of the conditional syntax of the LXX, see Anwar Tjen, *On Conditionals in the Greek Pentateuch: A Study of Translation Syntax* (Library of Hebrew Bible/Old Testament Studies 515; New York; London: T. & T. Clark, 2010).

17. Schiffman, "The Laws of Vows and Oaths," 200–201.

must take heed to perform").[18] After citing Deut 23:24, the author immediately moves to a discussion of the binding oaths in Num 30:3–16.[19] Even
though the *Damascus Document* cites the first half of v. 24 of Deuteronomy's law of vows, the author seems to read נדבה ["freewill offering"]
from the second half of v. 24 as a reference to oaths, rather than vows.[20]
Schiffman suggests that vows may have been "expunged" from the law by
the author of the *Damascus Document* and concludes that the "Zadokite"
community may have rejected vows all together.[21]

Schiffman's position is contrasted by Joseph M. Baumgarten, who argues that the *Damascus Document* conflates oaths and vows or reads them
as synonymous terms.[22] The important point for my argument is that the
sort of ambiguity we encounter regarding distinctions between vows and
oaths in the Second Temple period suggests that vows and oaths were not
yet systematically and uniformly distinguished.[23] It is precisely this lack
of consensus and confusion regarding the distinction between oaths and
vows that accounts for the proliferation of Second Temple interpretations
of the relevant biblical passages.

---

18. The *Damascus Document* (including the Genizah and Qumran manuscripts) does
not cite the initial law of Deut 23:22 regarding vows, nor does it the immediately following negation or antithesis (Deut 23:23), but it does cite the continuation and conclusion
of the law of vows (Deut 23:24; CD 16:6–7/4Q271 4 ii 7–8). See Joseph M. Baumgarten,
Qumran Cave 4. XIII: The Damascus Document (4Q266–273) (DJD 18; Oxford: Clarendon,
1996) 178–80. For the Genizah manuscripts, see Magen Broshi, ed., *The Damascus Document
Reconsidered* (Jerusalem: Israel Exploration Society, 1992) 40–41.

19. The *Damascus Document* does make an adjustment to the Hebrew of its base text,
adding "*le-haqim*," which is "intended to clarify the ambiguous *we-ʿasita* of Deuteronomy"
(Schiffman, "The Laws of Vows and Oaths," 201). According to Schiffman, "the problem
with this word in the MT is determining whether it is part of the preceding clause or that
which follows. Our text from the *Zadokite Fragments* clearly takes it as part of the first
clause, in agreement with the Masoretic accents. Yet one cannot help but note," Schiffman
continues, "that a surface reading of the text would see this verb as serving the clause which
follows. To avoid such an interpretation, the *Zadokite Fragments* passage adds *le-haqim* at
this point" (ibid.).

20. Ibid.

21. Ibid., 212.

22. Joseph M. Baumgarten points out that CD 16:10, in its reference to vows in Num
30:4, uses "the rubric על שבועת האשה" (Baumgarten, *Damascus Document*, 66). One could
argue in either direction—Schiffman's or Baumgarten's—that CD either eliminates vowing
altogether, or that it conflates vows and oaths.

23. In an article in which he argues that Jesus prohibited all oaths, John P. Meier suggests that, although "both Judaism and Christianity slowly developed clear definitions and
classifications of oaths and vows, . . . such clarity is not to be presumed around the time of
Jesus" ("Did the Historical Jesus Prohibit All Oaths? Part 1," *JSHJ* 5 [2007] 175–204 [at
p. 178]). Jonathan Klawans, in his response to Meier's article, accepts "that the distinction
between oaths and vows is insufficiently drawn, and not well enough attested, to be of great
use" ("The Prohibition of Oaths and Contra-Scriptural *Halakhot*: A Response to John P.
Meier," *JSHJ* 6 [2008] 33–48 [at p. 34]).

The view that all vows are illegitimate, as the Temple Scroll and the *Damascus Document* both testify, is indicative of Second Temple reservations about the wisdom of vowing and oath-taking. Philo also expressed reservations about both practices.[24] This Second Temple milieu helps explain the motivation for the interpolation in Deuteronomy's law of vows. The interpolator was religiously opposed to vowing: so strongly did he wish to discourage the widespread traditional practice that, mirroring the language of the tradition, he added a correction to the tradition to discourage the practice. Later on, the Matthean Jesus would similarly take a stand against traditional religious practice in regard to vows and oaths: "Again, you have heard that it was said to those of ancient times, 'You shall not swear falsely, but carry out the vows you have made to the Lord.' But I say to you, Do not swear at all" (Matt 5:33–37; NRSV). Here too the correction of the tradition, now explicitly identified as such, given the sharp antithesis, follows the citation of the tradition. Dennis C. Duling uses numismatic evidence and passages from Josephus to build a case for the origin of the Matthean Jesus' "anti-oath" formula as a response to the rule of Herod Agrippa I (37–44 C.E.).[25] I suggest, however, that Matthew may be drawing on a much larger textual tradition of Second Temple–period hesitation about the wisdom of vowing.

Once the correction of the tradition took place in Deuteronomy, it created a disordered text that caused Second Temple readers to stumble over the intrusive clause. The disruption led not only to the exegetical innovations of the Temple Scroll composer but also to Qoheleth's rearrangement of the law's content. It is to Qoheleth that we now turn.

III. Qoheleth's Revision and Reworking of Deuteronomy's Law of Vows

Qoheleth offers an especially important example of the Second Temple interpretation of pentateuchal passages dealing with vowing, because it actually reorders Deuteronomy's law of vows. Deuteronomy's law of vows is

---

24. See also Philo, *Spec.* 2.1–9, §§2–38, for the rejection of oath and vow-taking. Texts that do not outright reject the validity of vowing but certainly question the wisdom of doing so—Prov 20:25 and Sir 18:22—should also be noted here.

25. Dennis C. Duling, "'[Do Not Swear . . .] by Jerusalem Because It Is the City of the Great King' (Matt 5:35)," *JBL* 110 (1991) 291–309. More persuasive is the approach taken by Reinhard Neudecker, *Moses Interpreted by the Pharisees and Jesus: Matthew's Antitheses in the Light of Early Rabbinic Literature* (SubBi 44; Rome: Gregorian & Biblical Press, 2012) 83–97. Neudecker adduces early Jewish evidence for restraint in pronouncing the Tetragrammaton, and that, therefore, discourages vows and oaths employing the divine name. He sees Jesus as sharpening that traditional standpoint.

taken up in Qoh 5:3–4, which is set within a larger unit (4:17–5:6). Often passed over by earlier scholars, the unit is now seen as the structural center of the book's composition because of the way it engages theological tradition.[26]

A strong case has been made for dating Qoheleth to the Hellenistic period.[27] Qoheleth was a philosophical empiricist who transformed a theological orientation toward the world into a view that was questioning and empirical. Thus, as Diethelm Michel argues, the connections to religious tradition in Qoheleth are primarily critical.[28] Similarly, Thomas Krüger regards Qoheleth as providing a critical-rationalist rereading and reevaluation of pentateuchal theological and legal norms ("kritisch reflektiert").[29] Krüger tries to break free of the standard dichotomy between piety and alleged rejection of religious traditions. He suggests instead that Qoheleth retains but relativizes these traditions, shifting their status from

---

26. Norbert Lohfink deserves credit for his instrumental role in recognizing the unit's function in the larger structure of the book (*Kohelet* [NEchtB; Stuttgart: Echter Verlag, 1989] 40). See further Izak J. J. Spangenberg, "A Century of Wrestling with Qohelet: The Research History of the Book Illustrated with a Discussion of Qoh 4,17–5,6," in *Qohelet in the Context of Wisdom* (ed. Antoon Schoors; BETL 136; Leuven: Leuven University Press and Peeters, 1998) 61–91 [at pp. 82–83]); and Antoon Schoors, "Introduction," in ibid., 2–4.

27. Antoon Schoors argues that the language of Qoheleth is representative of Late Biblical Hebrew and that it should be dated to the Hellenistic period. See his two-part study, *The Preacher Sought to Find Pleasing Words: A Study of the Language of Qoheleth* (OLA 41; Leuven: Peeters / Department of Oriental Studies, 1992) 221–24; and *The Preacher Sought to Find Pleasing Words: A Study of the Language of Qoheleth, Part II: Vocabulary* (OLA 143; Leuven: Peeters / Department of Oriental Studies, 2004) 499–502. For further confirmation of the Hellenistic dating, see Thomas Krüger, *Qoheleth: A Commentary* (trans. O. C. Dean Jr.; Hermeneia; Minneapolis: Fortress, 2004) 19–21. On linguistic and historical grounds, Krüger dates Qoheleth to ca. 250–200 B.C.E. In contrast, C. L. Seow argues for a Persian period date, from the second half of the fifth to the first half of the fourth centuries (*Ecclesiastes: A New Translation with Introduction and Commentary* [AB 18C; New York: Doubleday, 1997] 13–14, 20); and idem, "Linguistic Evidence and the Dating of Qohelet," *JBL* 115 (1996) 643–66.

28. Diethelm Michel, "'Unter der Sonne': Zur Immanenz bei Qohelet," in *Qohelet in the Context of Wisdom* (ed. Antoon Schoors; BETL 136; Leuven: Leuven University Press / Peeters, 1998) 93–111; idem, *Qohelet* (EdF 258; Darmstadt: Wissenschaftliche Buchgesellschaft, 1988) 143. From a different perspective, also stressing the function of the unit as critiquing "accepted religion," see Ruth Fidler, "Qoheleth in 'the House of God': Text and Intertext in Qoh 4:17–5:6 (Eng. 5:1–7)," *HS* 47 (2006) 7–21 (quoted at 21). Fidler argues the unit evokes the Jacob-Bethel tradition in order to subvert it. There is indeed intertextuality in Qoheleth, but the specifics involving subversion of the Jacob-Bethel tradition that Fidler argues for go beyond the evidence.

29. Thomas Krüger regards Qoheleth as typologically similar to the philosophers of the Enlightenment ("aufklärischen"), who critically examine the religious teachings of the past and treat the Bible less as an authoritative canon than as a classical text or resource ("Die Rezeption der Tora im Buch Kohelet," in *Kritische Weisheit: Studien zur weisheitlichen Traditionskritik im Alten Testament* [Zurich: Pano, 1997] 173–93 (at p. 193).

authoritatively binding because of their divine origin to persuasive to the extent that they are evident to and consistent with the exercise of reason. Often the divine origin of such norms is obscured in their reworking by Qoheleth, or the divine sanction for breach of the norms is replaced by an appeal to reason.

Along with recognizing the centrality of the unit in theological terms, scholars increasingly recognize Qoheleth's frequent quotation of earlier sources and consider how these citations function.[30] Michael Fox provides a helpful summary of the literary context in which the citations are embedded: "The main theme of the present unit is caution in making vows. The remarks about going to the Temple, offering sacrifices, avoiding rash speech, and fearing God are all organized around this theme and should be interpreted in this context."[31] Each of the three sections of the unit refers to the כסיל ("fool"), which serves as a *Leitwort*.[32] The author presents three major examples of cultic praxis—namely, sacrifice, verbose prayer, and the superficial swearing of vows—and identifies them as characteristic of fools. It is important to keep in mind that a biblical vow is not (contrary to modern use) simply an oral affirmation. A vow promises payment to God (usually a sacrifice at a temple) for granting a petitioner's request (see I Sam I:II). The vow represents a cultic act in Deuteronomy, where its contextual location is after the injunction not to bring "wages of a dog" into the temple (Deut 23:19). The law of vows is also placed in a cultic context in Qoheleth. As Krüger notes, "The independent position of the text [Qoh 4:17–5:6] is especially recognizable in the way in which it substantiates and motivates the recommended behavior in the cultic realm." While Qoh 5:3–4 cites Deuteronomy's law of vows, it does not do so because of the authority of Scripture as much as because of the law's reasonableness.[33] "Repeatedly serving as motivation for the 'proper' adoration of God is the distancing of oneself from the behavior of 'fools.'"[34] It is in this context that Qoheleth cites and revises the law of vows in Deuteronomy.[35]

Qoheleth cites and reworks Deuteronomy's law of vows as shown in fig. 2.2.[36]

---

30. Spangenberg credits Robert Gordis for originally suggesting that Qoheleth contains actual quotations of wisdom sayings (Spangenberg, "A Century of Wrestling with Qohelet," 71; and Gordis, *Koheleth: The Man and His World* [The Jewish Theological Seminary of America 19; New York: Bloch, 1955] 236, 238).

31. Michael Fox, *Ecclesiastes: The Traditional Hebrew Text with the New JPS Translation and Commentary* (Philadelphia: Jewish Publication Society, 2004) 32.

32. Michel, "Unter der Sonne," 105.

33. Krüger, "Die Rezeption der Tora im Buch Kohelet," 177.

34. Idem, *Qoheleth*, 111.

35. Fox, *Ecclesiastes*, 32.

36. The layout of fig. 2.2 is patterned after Michel, "Unter der Sonne," 107–8.

Deut 23:22	כי <u>תדר נדר ליהוה אלהיך</u> <u>לא תאחר לשלמו</u>	
Qoh 5:3	כאשר <u>תדר נדר</u> לאלהים <u>אל תאחר לשלמו</u>	
Deut 23:22 (cont.)	כי דרש ידרשנו יהוה אלהיך מעמך והיה בך חטא	
Qoh 5:3 (cont.)	<u>כי</u> אין חפץ בכסילים את אשר תדר שלם	

Deut 23:22	<u>If you make a vow to</u> Yahweh your <u>God, do not delay in fulfilling it,</u>
Qoh 5:3	When <u>you make a vow to</u> God, do <u>not delay in fulfilling it,</u>
Deut 23:22 (cont.)	<u>for</u> Yahweh your God will surely require it of you, and it will count against you as a sin.
Qoh 5:3 (cont.)	<u>for</u> there is no delight in fools. What you vow, fulfill.

FIGURE 2.2. Qoheleth's Transformation of the
Initial Admonition in Deuteronomy's Law of Vows

As indicated by the underlining, there is near-verbatim correspondence between the opening verses in Deuteronomy and Qoheleth (Deut 23:22/Qoh 5:3).[37] But Qoheleth did not simply cite Deuteronomy as some sort of proof text or as an immutable authority to back its own agenda.[38]

---

37. Also noting the nearly identical wording, see Ludger Schwienhorst-Schönberger, *Kohelet* (Herders Theologischer Kommentar zum Alten Testament; Freiburg: Herder, 2004) 315.

38. Michel also recognizes the textual dependence of Qoheleth on Deuteronomy ("Unter der Sonne," 93–111); see also Norbert Lohfink, "Warum ist der Tor unfähig, böse zu handeln [Koh 4,17]," *Studien zu Kohelet* (SBAB 26; Stuttgart: Katholisches Bibelwerk, 1998) 82–94 (at p. 90 n. 34); and idem, *Qoheleth* (trans. Sean McEvenue; CC; Minneapolis: Fortress, 2003) 77. Franz Delitzsch was among the first to show how Qoheleth represents "in Gedanken und Ausdruck das Echo von Dt. 23,22–24" (*Hoheslied und Koheleth* [Leipzig: Dörffling und Franke, 1875] 287). Despite the near-verbatim correspondence, it has been argued that there is no literary dependence between the two texts. Moshe Weinfeld claimed that Deuteronomy's law of vows is "distinctly sapiential in character and we need not assume that the passage in Ecclesiastes is dependent upon it" (*Deuteronomy and the Deuteronomic School* [Oxford: Clarendon, 1972] 270). Weinfeld sees Deuteronomy's law of vows as dependent, not on the literary text of Qoheleth, but on a shared wisdom tradition that is reflected in Qoheleth (pp. 270–71). In actuality, the verbatim correspondence between the two texts is so specific that it is best explained in terms of literary dependence, a dependence that could only run in one direction: from Deuteronomy to Qoheleth. For a thoughtful response that addresses other methodological issues with Weinfeld's argument for the sapiential influence on Deuteronomy, see Christianus Brekelmans, "Wisdom Influence in Deuteronomy," in *A Song of Power and the Power of Song: Essays on the Book of Deuteronomy* (ed. Duane L. Christensen; Sources for Biblical and Theological Study 3; Winona Lake, IN: Eisenbrauns, 1993) 123–34.

Instead, Qoheleth revised and reworked the law of vows, thereby undermining Deuteronomy's theological rationale for fulfilling vows.[39] The command to fulfill vows promptly and the concession that it is better not to vow (Qoh 5:3–4) are very similar to the terms of the law of vows in Deut 23:22–23. The transformation, however, should be stressed: the law of vows is not cited as a divine command or as Torah legislation but as instruction by Qoheleth himself.[40] Similarly, breach of the teaching is no longer presented as a sin that mandates divine punishment (as in Deut 23:22) but as foolishness that is merely displeasing to God.[41] In this way, the Torah's absolute prohibition (using the prohibitive in Deut 23:22) is relativized by Qoheleth to a mere transgression against the dictates of wisdom and good sense.[42]

The textual changes and interventions in Qoheleth range from linguistic updating to substantive theological transformations.

1. Linguistic updating of the syntax of conditions is the first significant change. The original protasis marker used in classical pentateuchal law, כי, *if*, is replaced by the temporal conjunction, כאשר, *when*. Whereas the former has a range of meanings in different contexts, the latter is unambiguous as a temporal marker and was increasingly used throughout the Second Temple period.[43]

2. Qoheleth also changes Deuteronomy's prohibitive לא to vetitive אל.[44]

---

39. Contra Otto Kaiser, who has claimed that Qoheleth was pious and consistent with Deuteronomic theology ("Die Botschaft des Buches Kohelet," *ETL* 71 [1995] 48–70 [at p. 64]). Kaiser has been followed by his student, Alexander A. Fischer, *Skepsis oder Furcht Gottes? Studien zur Komposition und Theologie des Buches Kohelet* (BZAW 247; Berlin: de Gruyter, 1996) 48. More persuasive is the position of Diethelm Michel, who rejects the position of Kaiser and Fischer. Michel demonstrates that the notion that the citation points to an alleged Second Temple Jewish *Gesetzesfrömmigkeit* ("piety toward the law") is untenable ("Unter der Sonne," 105–8; idem, *Qohelet* [EdF 258; Darmstadt: Wissenschaftliche Buchgesellschaft, 1988] 72). Michel recognizes the dialectical nature of the citation of Scripture, which is interested not in piety and consistency with tradition but, rather, in the inversion of tradition. Previously, Wilhelm Rudolph noted that Qoheleth, although he stood in the same tradition as Ben Sira and Proverbs, often cited tradition in order to polemicize against it (*Vom Buch Kohelet: Vortrag, gehalten anlässlich des Rektoratsantritts am 12. November 1958* [Münster: Aschendorff, 1959] 11).

40. Krüger, "Die Rezeption der Tora im Buch Kohelet," 177–78.

41. Ibid.

42. Ibid.

43. See part 1 of this book, p. 10.

44. Antoon Schoors suggests that "the alteration of the particle of negation לא into אל betrays an alteration of genre: Deuteronomy gives a legal prohibition in an apodictic style, whereas Qoheleth's expression is an instruction and comes close to a piece of advice"

3. Consistent with Qoheleth's general avoidance of the Tetra-grammaton, both occurrences in the law of vows are deleted, as is Deuteronomy's אלהיך ("your God"), which makes a hom-iletic appeal to the addressee. In their place, Qoheleth employs the more neutral form, אלהים ("God").[45]

4. Qoheleth rewrites the motive clause in Deuteronomy's law of vows, with its theological rationale ("for Yahweh your God will surely require it of you, and it will count against you as a sin"). He replaces the divine subject of the clause with an objective formulation with an indefinite subject: "for there is no delight in fools," which makes no mention of God, let alone divine punishment for sin.[46] Instead of the religious significance of the vow to God, breach of which is sin against the deity, the focus becomes something closer to avoiding empty promises, such as fools are inclined to make.[47] The gravity of making a vow and failing to perform it is here removed from the realm of religion and cult and shifted into the domain of moral prag-matism and empiricism.[48]

Ancient interpreters have long sensed this attempt by Qoheleth to "de-theologize" the pentateuchal formulation. What Qoheleth removed to make a more objective statement, כי אין חפץ בכסילים, "for there is no de-light in fools" (Qoh 5:3b), is restored by the author of *Tg. Qoheleth*, who reinserts the deity's name into the motive clause, once again making the desire not to sin against the deity the primary rationale for honoring one's vows: ארום בגין כן לא רעוא מן קדם ייי בטפשיא, "for the LORD has no delight in fools." In effect, the targum here "re-theologizes" Qoheleth, align-ing and harmonizing it with its textual source in the Deuteronomic law of vows.[49]

(*Preacher, Part II*, 104). See also Elisha Qimron, *The Hebrew of the Dead Sea Scrolls* (HSS 29; Atlanta: Scholars Press, 1986) 80–81; and Jean-Sébastien Rey, "Quelques particularités lin-guistiques communes à 4QInstruction et à Ben Sira," in *Conservatism and Innovation in the Hebrew Language of the Hellenistic Period: Proceedings of a Fourth International Symposium on the Hebrew of the Dead Sea Scrolls & Ben Sira* (ed. Jan Joosten and Jean-Sébastien Rey; STDJ 73; Leiden: Brill, 2008) 155–74 (at p. 157). Ahouva Shulman does not take into account the law of vows ("The Function of the 'Jussive' and 'Indicative' Imperfect Forms in Biblical Hebrew Prose," *ZAH* 13 [2000] 168–80).

45. Michel, "Unter der Sonne," 108.

46. Idem, *Qohelet*, 143.

47. Ibid.

48. Idem, "Unter der Sonne," 108.

49. For the Aramaic text of the *Tg. Qoh*. 5:3, see Madeleine Taradach and Joan Ferrer, *Un Targum de Qohélet: Ms. M-2 de Salamanca, Editio princeps—Texte araméen, traduction et commentaire critique* (MdB 37; Geneva: Labor & Fides, 1998) 42. Ironically, some modern

One aspect of Qoheleth's reworking of the law of vows has escaped previous notice. Qoheleth implicitly recognized the textual disorder in Deuteronomy's law of vows and sought to correct it. After transforming Deuteronomy's motive clause, Qoheleth proceeded to invert the order of Deuteronomy's text precisely at the site where I propose that the original order of the law was disturbed by an interpolation. Qoheleth reorders the law's original sequence from A B C to A C' B':

Deut 23:22–24a	Qoh 5:3–4
כי תדר נדר ליהוה אלהיך לא תאחר לשלמו	כאשר תדר נדר לאלהים אל תאחר לשלמו
כי דרש ידרשנו יהוה אלהיך מעמך והיה בך חטא	כי אין חפץ בכסילים
וכי תחדל לנדר לא יהיה בך חטא	את אשר תדר שלם
מוצא שפתיך תשמר ועשית	טוב אשר לא תדר משתדור ולא תשלם
If you make a vow to Yahweh your God, do not delay in fulfilling it, **A**	When you make a vow to God, do not delay in fulfilling it, **A**
for Yahweh your God will surely require it of you, and it will count against you as a sin.	for there is no delight in fools.
But if you refrain from vowing, **B** it will not count against you as a sin.	What you vow, fulfill. **C'**
What has gone forth from your lips **C** you must take heed to perform.	Better that you should not vow **B'** than to vow and not fulfill.

FIGURE 2.3. Qoheleth's Reordering of Deuteronomy's Law of Vows

In addition to inverting the order, Qoheleth paraphrases Deuteronomy's "What has gone forth from your lips you must take heed to perform" (C),

---

scholars unconsciously make the same theological harmonization. Norbert Lohfink's rendering, "Die Ungebildeten gefallen Gott nicht," is closer to the midrash haggadah of the targum at this point than to a literal translation (*Kohelet*, 41). Lohfink makes a similar move in his English commentary. After noting how Qoheleth follows Deuteronomy "verbatim in part," Lohfink continues: "He changes only one thing: he transfers to v. 5 the statement of Deuteronomy [23:22] that God would consider a vow made and not fulfilled to be a sin involving guilt worthy of death, and thereby he connects it to the unallowable *šĕgāgâ* declaration. In place of this statement he introduces the following, regarding the vow: 'God takes no delight in the fool.'" Lohfink astutely notices both the textual dependence and the textual reordering on the part of Qoheleth, but there are a number of problems with the details of his analysis: (1) the precise claim that Qoheleth "transfers to v. 5 the statement of Deuteronomy" concerning "sin" necessarily relies on a single shared word, "sin," but there is no other connection, lexical or otherwise, between Deut 23:22 and Qoh 5:5; (2) at no point in Deuteronomy's law of vows or in Qoheleth's reworking is there any expressed notion of unfulfilled vowing as a "sin involving guilt *worthy of death*" (emphasis mine); (3) Lohfink reinserts "God" where Qoheleth had deleted the Tetragrammaton and replaced it with the negative particle of existence, אין (*Qoheleth*, 76–77).

yielding a more terse "What you vow, fulfill" (C'). Qoheleth also replaces Deuteronomy's alternative or negative condition, "But if you refrain from vowing, it will not count against you as a sin" (B), with a "better that" saying: "Better that you should not vow than to vow and not fulfill" (B'). In the process of inverting the order of Deuteronomy, Qoheleth yields a more logical and coherent sequence. This solution is strikingly similar to what we saw earlier in Marti's paraphrase. Qoheleth reorders the law of vows so that the encouragement to refrain from vowing (B) no longer disrupts the continuity between the two verses concerned with fulfilling vows once they are made (A and C). Instead, the admonition to abstain from vowing concludes the unit, thus receiving the emphasis. The restoration of the more logical order of the content of Deuteronomy's law of vows suggests that Qoheleth read the law as a disordered text. This sort of disorder is indicative of an interpolation. I shall now turn to an analysis of the *Sipre*, which also deals with Qoheleth and its reading of the law of vows.

IV. The Reception of the Law of Vows in Sipre Deuteronomy *and Rabbinic Literature*

The history of interpretation provides further evidence that various Jewish communities in antiquity found it difficult to read Deuteronomy's law of vows as a coherent unit, let alone as an intelligible statement of what one should or should not do. It is very difficult to find any context in which the law is seen as offering an integrated approach to the problem of vowing or where its two main injunctions are seen as compatible. Instead, it is as though the law of vows became a sort of Rorschach blot onto which the competing currents in social history, for or against vowing, mapped their positions. The major Tannaitic legal commentary on the book of Deuteronomy, *Sipre Deuteronomy*, shows the two countervailing positions clearly, as is clear in fig. 2.4.[50]

---

50. Dating *Sipre Deuteronomy* is difficult. According to Steven D. Fraade, "[I]t is generally thought to draw its traditions from the teachings of the Palestinian rabbinic sages from ca. 70–ca. 230 C.E., but to have been editorially composed in its present form probably a generation or two later (mid- to late third century)" ("Deuteronomy in Sifre to Deuteronomy," in *Encyclopaedia of Midrash: Biblical Interpretation in Formative Judaism* [ed. Jacob Neusner and Alan J. Avery-Peck; Leiden: Brill, 2005] 1:54–59 [at p. 54]).

The text of *Siphre Deuteronomy* is from Louis Finkelstein, *Siphre on Deuteronomy* (New York: Jewish Theological Seminary, 1969) 286 (*pisqa* §265). For the standard translation, see Reuven Hammer, *Sifre: A Tannaitic Commentary on the Book of Deuteronomy* (Yale Judaica Series 24; New Haven: Yale University Press, 1986) 261. Note the parallel at *b. Ḥullin* 2a.

> (כג) וכי תחדל לנדור, רבי מאיר טוב אשר לא תדור משתדור
> ולא תשלם טוב מזה ומזה שלא תדור כל עיקר רבי יהודה אומר טוב אשר לא
> תדור טוב מזה ומזה נודר ומשלם.
>
> *But if you refrain from vowing* (Deut 23:23):
>   R. Meir cites: *Better that you should not vow than that you vow and
> not fulfill* (Qoh 5:4). Still better than either this alternative or that alter-
> native is that *you should not vow* at all.
>   R. Judah, however, cites: *Better that you should not vow* (Qoh 5:4a).
> Still better than either this alternative or that alternative is vowing
> and paying.

FIGURE 2.4. The Debate on the Law of Vows
in *Sipre Deuteronomy*

The terms of the debate are not easy to follow because of the density
of the rabbinic dialectic. The context is not provided, the positions are ar-
ticulated only laconically, and the citations of the biblical text are, charac-
teristically, not provided fully. But working through the rabbinic reasoning
allows one to sense the pungency of their conclusions.[51]

Both R. Meir and R. Judah are concerned with understanding Deut
23:23: "But if you do not vow, it will not count as a sin against you." In
effect, they are asking how this verse fits in its context. Specifically, how
does it relate to the preceding admonition, "If you make a vow to Yahweh
your God, do not delay in fulfilling it, for Yahweh your God will require
it of you, and it will count against you as a sin" (Deut 23:22)? In order to
answer their question, each sage turns to Qoheleth.[52] If we attempt to look
at it from their perspective, Qoheleth's formulation contains three separate
halakic positions (see fig. 2.5).

Qoheleth is a dialectical thinker. He articulates three separate possible
courses of action in regard to vowing, without himself ever taking a clear
position on one of the issues. Although he maintains that it is better not
to vow than to vow and not fulfill, he never addresses whether it is better
to incur divine favor by vowing and paying or to avoid vowing altogether

---

51. On the dialogical nature of the rabbinic debates in the *Sipre*, see Steven D. Fraade,
*From Tradition to Commentary: Torah and Its Interpretation in the Midrash Sifre to Deu-
teronomy* (SUNY Series in Judaica: Hermeneutics, Mysticism, and Religion; Albany: State
University of New York, 1991).

52. They do so on the basis of an implicit exegetical analogy, *gezerah shava*, since the
phrase נדר תדר appears in both Deut 22:22 and Qoh 3:4. On *gezerah shava*, see Saul J. Lieberman, *Hellenism in Jewish Palestine* (2nd ed.; New York: Jewish Theological Seminary of
America, 1962) 58–62; and Menahem Elon, *Jewish Law: History, Sources, Principles* (4 vols.;
Philadelphia: Jewish Publication Society, 1994) 1:351–55.

Qoh 5:3–4	*Halakic Conclusion Drawn*
כאשר תדר נדר לאלהים אל תאחר לשלמו . . . את אשר תדר שלם	
טוב אשר לא תדר	
משתדור ולא תשלם	
[3] When you make a vow to God, do not delay in fulfilling it. . . . What you vow, fulfill.	I. *Vowing and paying*
[4a] Better that you should not vow	II. *Not vowing [and therefore not paying]*
[4b] than that you vow and not fulfill.	III. *Vowing and not paying*

FIGURE 2.5. Reconstruction of
Sipre Deuteronomy's Reading of Qoh 5:3–4

and thereby remain free of the slightest risk of incurring divine displeasure. This is the issue addressed by the rabbinic discussion.

After citing Qoh 5:4, R. Meir contends, טוב מזה ומזה, "Still better than either this alternative [I: vowing and paying] or that alternative [III: vowing and not paying] is that *you should not vow at all* [alternative II]." Using the same proof text, R. Judah reaches the opposite conclusion: טוב מזה ומזה, "Still better than either this alternative [II: not vowing] or that alternative [III: vowing and not paying] is *vowing and paying* [alternative I]. R. Meir's position reflects the urge to avoid vows altogether. In effect, R. Meir is anchoring the rabbinic hesitations about the wisdom of vowing on Deut 23:23, which here becomes a proof text and a general statement that the wisest course of action in religious life (טוב מזה ומזה) is: "You should not vow כל עיקר *at all*." With this כל עיקר, which makes the statement an absolute and unconditional admonition, R. Meir has deftly silenced Deut 23:22 altogether. Instead, Deut 23:23 is read as an independent admonition. There is no longer any consideration given to vowing. Or, to put it differently, the intrusive v. 23 has here trumped the preceding admonition to fulfill one's vows (v. 22).

In contrast to this, the position of R. Judah is remarkably conservative: it becomes something like a bastion that seeks to maintain fidelity to pentateuchal law and the textual status quo. In affirming that it is best (טוב מזה ומזה) to *vow and pay*, in effect he posits v. 23 as a subcondition and asserts the primacy of Deut 23:22, "If you make a vow to Yahweh your God, do not delay in paying it." R. Judah is reading this verse as an absolute good. In effect, he is trying to silence the following verse, the alternative of refraining from vowing. One might go so far as to suggest that, at the level of exegesis, he attempts text-critical surgery on the law of vows, removing the problematic interpolation in order to read the law coherently.

The most striking aspect of the exegetical debate on vowing (Deut 23:22) or not vowing (Deut 23:23) is that the debate needs to be held at all. Normally, rabbinic legal exegesis has no trouble dealing with redundant, inconsistent, or even contradictory texts. According to the system of harmonistic legal exegesis (midrash halakah), the simple solution is to deny any redundancy, inconsistency, or contradiction.[53] In the case of the three pentateuchal manumission laws, for example, each is construed as having a separate application so that there is no overlap between them. Theoretically, a similar approach might have worked here: "*If you vow*: this applies to case A. *But if you do not vow*: this applies to case B." But no such solution is suggested. Instead, the text becomes a context for arguing the relative merits of vowing or not vowing. Neither R. Meir nor R. Judah can read Deuteronomy's law of vows as a coherent unit; each must choose between v. 22 and v. 23, between vowing and not vowing, and between the original text and the interpolation.

This debate on vows struck a responsive chord in a wide range of rabbinic texts. It is widely cited in both the Babylonian and the Palestinian Talmuds in a number of contexts.[54] The position of R. Meir seems to become dominant, to the extent that the very notion of vowing altogether comes to be regarded as a sin:

> It is taught by Rav Dimi, brother of Rav Safra: Anyone who makes a vow, even if he carries it out, is called a sinner. Rav Zevid said: What biblical passage proves this? "*If you refrain* from vowing, it will not count as a sin against you" (Deut 23:23). This means: *If you do not refrain*, then there is a sin.[55]

---

53. On rabbinic interpretive approaches to Scripture, see Louis Jacobs and David Derovan, "Hermeneutics," in *Encyclopaedia Judaica* (22 vols.; 2nd ed.; Detroit: Macmillan, 2007) 9:25–29. The assumption about the coherence and nonredundancy of Scripture is shared by nearly all ancient Jewish exegetes, as noted by James Kugel, "Early Jewish Biblical Interpretation," in *The Eerdmans Dictionary of Early Judaism* (ed. John J. Collins and Daniel C. Harlow; Grand Rapids, MI: Eerdmans, 2010) 121–41 (at p. 132); and Bernard M. Levinson, "The Case for Revision and Interpolation within the Biblical Legal Corpora," *"The Right Chorale": Studies in Biblical Law and Interpretation* (FAT 54; Tübingen: Mohr Siebeck, 2008) 201–23 (at p. 222).

54. See Finkelstein, *Siphre on Deuteronomy*, 286 (*pisqa* §265).

55. *B. Ned.* 77b; similarly, *b. Ned.* 22a. Adapted from Gaby Barzilai, "Women's Vows," http://www.biu.ac.il/JH/Parasha/eng/matot/bar1.html [accessed 17 December 2012].

The assumption here is that the vow is an unconditional religious wrong-doing, precisely because commitments made to the deity are absolute. The potential for calamity associated with careless vowing is especially evident in the story of Jephthah in Judg 11:29–40. The tendency to limit vowing becomes so strong that the definition of sin in the source text of the law of vows—failure to fulfill the vow punctually—is simply set aside. Now it is vowing itself that incurs sin. This sort of position receives extensive attention: "One who vows is as though he has built a *bamah* [high place for unlawful sacrifice], and if he fulfills it [i.e., the vow] is as though he has sacrificed on it."[56] From this perspective, vowing becomes an act of apostasy, and the paying of the vow, contrary to Deuteronomy's admonition, merely heightens the apostasy, as if it were an act of false worship.

This circumspection toward the wisdom of vowing is especially evident in *Kol Nidrei* ("All Vows"), which is recited on the eve of the Day of Atonement; the petitioner declares that all personal vows made during the past year should be considered null and void. The reference to the past year arises from rabbinic exegesis of our verse, where the admonition "Do not delay in fulfilling it" is parsed to mean within the annual cycle of the three pilgrimage festivals. Technically, the *Kol Nidrei* proclamation is not a prayer, since it does not address God, and the deity is nowhere referenced in it. Indeed, the proclamation was opposed by the talmudic academies of both Sura and Pumbedita.[57] This solemn petition recognizes the importance of the law of vows and seeks extralegal redress for vows made to God but not fulfilled.

We have seen in this section how the ancient Tannaim whose voices are preserved in *Sipre Deuteronomy* struggled with Deuteronomy's law of vows. Their difficulty in reading the text as a coherent composition and then deriving two antithetical positions from it points to an implicit recognition that there was a textual disturbance. In what follows, I take a closer look at Deuteronomy's law of vows and, in the process, build a case for an interpolation as the cause of the disordered sequence.

V. The Anomalous Sequence of Conditional Legal Statements in Deuteronomy's Law of Vows

Deut 23:23 not only disrupts the logical order of the content between vv. 22 and 24 but also disrupts the legal syntax of the law. The particular

---

56. *B. Ned.* 22a (R. Nathan).

57. As Peter Lenhardt notes, "[T]he declaration dates from the geonic period and persisted despite the opposition of almost all leading ge'onim, *ri'shonim,* and *aharonim*" ("Kol Nidrei," *The Oxford Dictionary of the Jewish Religion* [ed. R. J. Zwi Werblowsky and Geoffrey Wigoder; Oxford: Oxford University Press, 1997] 404–5).

combination of casuistically formulated laws (vv. 22 and 23) that consists of protasis-marking כי in A (v. 22) followed by protasis-marking וכי in B (v. 23) creates an anomalous sequence of conditional legal statements. This formulation is irregular in two respects: (1) Except for the contrasting case of the manumission law, as we shall see, there is no case in the legal corpus of Deuteronomy of two laws arranged in this sequence of כי + וכי; (2) There is no other sequence of two laws in which the second law reverses and negates both the protasis and the apodosis of the preceding law and represents its complete antithesis.

A [22]	כי תדר נדר ליהוה אלהיך לא תאחר לשלמו כי דרש ידרשנו יהוה אלהיך מעמך והיה בך חטא
B [23]	וכי תחדל לנדר לא יהיה בך חטא
C [24]	מוצא שפתיך תשמר ועשית כאשר נדרת ליהוה אלהיך נדבה אשר דברת בפיך
A [22]	If you make a vow to Yahweh your God, you must not delay in fulfilling it, for Yahweh your God will surely require it of you, and it will count against you as a sin.
B [23]	But if you refrain from vowing, it will not count against you as a sin.
C [24]	What has gone forth from your lips you must take heed to perform, just as you have vowed to Yahweh your God as a freewill offering, which you have promised by your mouth.

FIGURE 2.6. Order of Conditionals in
Deuteronomy's Law of Vows (Deut 23:22–24)

Along with the redactor of the Temple Scroll, who as we have seen grammatically instantiated v. 23 as a subcondition, a number of modern scholars have implicitly recognized and accounted for the awkward sequence of the law by reading the conditional clause at the problematic point (v. 23), where the protasis is marked by וכי as being a formal subcondition. Subconditions address variations or complications of the main conditional or casuistic law. When v. 23 is read as a formal subcondition—an elaboration, variation, or complication of the immediately preceding law—it ostensibly becomes a digression, allowing v. 24 to be construed as the resumption of the main law in v. 22. Reading v. 23 as a subcondition would, then, conceivably allow the entire law (vv. 22–24) to be read as a coherent unit, thus eliminating any potential claim of interpolation.

Similar to what we saw in the Temple Scroll, attempts to account for the awkward syntax and sequence of the law of vows are largely driven by the harmonization of the specific rules governing conditionals in the Covenant Code (Exodus 21–23) with the legal syntax of Deuteronomy's legal code. Here I shall show that the modern attempts to read v. 23 as a subcondition do not resolve the textual difficulty, but—just as with the Temple Scroll—point to the underlying textual problem.

In an implicit attempt to impose some order on a disordered text, Gottfried Seitz has posited an internally consistent chiastic structure for the unit, reading v. 23 as a formal subcondition. Figure 2.7 shows Seitz's proposed chiasm for the law of vows.[58]

כי תדר נדר ליהוה אלהיך	If you make a vow to Yahweh your God,	A
לא תאחר לשלמו	do not delay in fulfilling it;	B
כי דרש ידרשנו יהוה אלהיך מעמך	for Yahweh your God will surely require it of you,	
והיה בך חטא	and it will count against you as a sin.	C
וכי תחדל לנדר	But if you refrain from vowing,	X
לא יהיה בך חטא	it will not count against you as a sin.	C'
מוצא שפתיך תשמר ועשית	What has gone forth from your lips you must take heed to perform,	B'
כאשר נדרת ליהוה אלהיך נדבה	just as you have vowed to Yahweh your God as a freewill offering,	A'
אשר דברת בפיך	which you have promised by your mouth.	

FIGURE 2.7. Seitz's Proposed Chiastic Structure
of Deuteronomy's Law of Vows

Seitz refers to v. 23's וכי תחדל לנדר לא יהיה בך חטא (X and C' in fig. 2.7) as a subcondition (*der Unterfall*) and notes how it refers back to the

---

58. Gottfried Seitz, *Redaktionsgeschichtliche Studien zum Deuteronomium* (BWANT 93; Stuttgart: Kohlhammer, 1971) 177–78. Although Seitz classifies the law of vows as a "'Wenn-du'-Gesetze," he postulates a chiastic structure analogous to that of Deut 15:1–3 and 23:20–21, which are both formulated in apodictic terms (p. 177 [also see pp. 167–68, 175–76]). The diagram is based on p. 178. I have added the translation as well as the letter headings (i.e., ABCXC'B'A').

apodosis of the preceding declaratory formula (B and C) because it claims that there is no offense in not vowing.[59] C and C' are certainly parallel and sandwich the protasis of the subcondition (X) at the center of the chiasmus. Following the subcondition, C', B', and A' resume the main law (A, B, C) by way of inverted repetition. However, a closer look at Seitz's arguments reveals that they are internally inconsistent. The alleged symmetries keep changing their terms: in one case, they are lexical (A and A'); in another, topical (B and B'). Furthermore, according to the proposed chiastic structure, כי דרש ידרשנו יהוה אלהיך מעמך, "for Yahweh your God will surely require it of you," is simply unaccounted for, as is the end of v. 24, אשר דברת בפיך, "which you have promised with your mouth." In order to account for the latter, Seitz follows Carl Steuernagel and suggests that it is a gloss.[60]

Ironically, Seitz highlights the most problematic part of the law's present formulation. At the center of Seitz's alleged chiasm is the admonition not to vow (v. 23), which he has identified as a formal subcondition.[61] Like Seitz, Gerhard Liedke also identifies Deut 23:23 as a subcondition. Although Liedke does not devote much attention to the law of vows, he does like Seitz include it in (as being consistent with) the larger series of "If . . . you" (*Wenn-du*) laws.[62] In his discussion of the rules of the syntax of conditionals, Liedke notes that the normal rule is: "כי leitet den

---

59. Ibid., 177.

60. Steuernagel proposed that there was a gloss at the end of v. 24 (*Übersetzung und Erklärung der Bücher Deuteronomium und Josua*, 87; idem, *Das Deuteronomium*, 137–38). See also Bertholet, *Deuteronomium*, 74; Smith, *Book of Deuteronomy*, 275; and Hölscher, "Komposition und Ursprung des Deuteronomiums," 161–255 (at p. 214 n. 1). Steuernagel saw אשר דברת בפיך, "which you have promised by your mouth," as exterior to the construction ("außerhalb der Konstr.") and suggested that it is a gloss to מוצא שפתיך, "what has gone forth from your lips" (*Das Deuteronomium*, 138). Steuernagel also suggested that the language there may be colored by the terminology used by P in the beginning of the vows unit in Numbers (specifically in 30:3; ibid., 137–38; idem, *Übersetzung und Erklärung*, 87). However, the only lexical connection between the two passages is the occurrence of מפיו, "from his mouth," in the vows unit of Num 30:3 and בפיך, "by your mouth," in Deuteronomy's law of vows (23:24). If there is a gloss at the end of v. 24, it cannot be adequately explained in terms of this sole lexical similarity, thus diminishing the likelihood of the gloss's being the work of P.

61. A. D. H. Mayes follows Seitz's proposed chiastic structure. Mayes recognizes that the law of vows "follows the pattern of the immediately preceding law [vv. 19–20], viz., a central phrase (v. 22) which is antithetical to the two parallel first and third elements (vv. 21, 23)" (*Deuteronomy* [NCB; London: Marshall, Morgan & Scott, 1979] 321).

62. See Gerhard Liedke, *Gestalt und Bezeichnung alttestamentlicher Rechtssätze: Eine formgeschichtlich-terminologische Studie* (WMANT 39; Neukirchen-Vluyn: Neukirchener Verlag, 1971) 21–22. His complete list includes: Deut 13:2–6, 7–12, 13–19; 15:12–18; 17:2–7 (8–13, 14–20); 21:10–14; 22:6–7, 8; 23:23–24, 25–26; 24:10–13, 19–22. For Seitz, see *Redaktionsgeschichtliche Studien*, 177.

Hauptfall ein, אם leitet Unterfälle ein" [כי is a main condition, and אם is a subcondition].[63] The problem is that the rule that Liedke alludes to does not explain the structure of the law of vows. According to Liedke's criteria, if Deut 23:23 is a subcondition, it should be marked by the use of אם, not, as is actually the case in v. 23, by the use of וכי. Liedke's criterion for a subcondition—that it be marked by אם—suggests that he has read the conditional (ו)כי of v. 23 as being functionally equivalent to אם.[64]

Now, one could quite reasonably ask whether the author of the law of vows simply used (ו)כי as a functional equivalent of אם. If (ו)כי is being used to mark a subcondition, then one would hope to find evidence elsewhere in Deuteronomy's legal corpus of this particular grammatical construction and its syntactical relationship with the rest of the law of vows. In order to determine if there is evidence of this sort, we must begin with a brief return to the Covenant Code's "hierarchical ordering of conditionals."

As discussed in part 1, the casuistic laws of the Covenant Code (i.e., Exod 21:2–22:16) use a unique system—termed "the hierarchical ordering of conditionals"—for separating units and for marking the difference between the main clause and the subconditions. The main law is always marked by use of conditional כי, while אם marks the subconditions. In comparison with the highly regulated system of the Covenant Code, the rules for using protasis-marking כי in the legal corpus of Deuteronomy are more varied.[65] There are three major types of change in Deuteronomy's legal corpus: (1) increased use of 2nd-person address;[66] (2) expansion of the use of כי to introduce a temporal clause (marking "when"), separate from its more conventional use to mark a hypothetical legal condition ("if");[67]

---

63. Liedke, *Gestalt und Bezeichnung alttestamentlicher Rechtssätze*, 31. Liedke cites Roderick A. F. Mackenzie, "The Formal Aspect of Ancient Near Eastern Law," in *The Seed of Wisdom: Essays in Honor of T. J. Meek* (ed. W. S. McCullough; Toronto: University of Toronto Press, 1964) 31–44 (at p. 35).

64. The use of conditional כי in the three different legal collections of the Pentateuch—the Covenant Code (Exodus 21–23), the legal corpus of Deuteronomy (Deuteronomy 12–26), and the Holiness Code (Leviticus 17–26)—is inconsistent (see part 1 of this book, p. 21 n. 64).

65. Udo Rüterswörden correctly recognizes that the legal syntax of Deuteronomy is distinct from that of the Covenant Code and that criteria valid for the Covenant Code do not apply to Deuteronomy ("Die Apodosis in den Rechtssätzen des Deuteronomiums," 130).

66. The rhetorical aims of the authors of the legal corpus have caused them to adjust the Covenant Code's casuistic 3rd-person "If . . . then" formula (Exod 21:2–22:16) in light of their goals of renewing, rethinking, and redefining the structure of their community and their relationship with their God. Parenesis is frequent and leads to extensive use of the distinctive כי + 2nd-person form ("If . . . you . . .").

67. Two cases introduce the distinctive *Landgabeformel* ("land-grant formula"). The first appears in Deut 17:14: כי תבא אל הארץ אשר יהוה אלהיך נתן לך, "*When* you enter the land

(3) changes in the structure of the legal paragraph. With the third change, instead of the כי clause's marking the beginning of the law, in a number of cases new units begin with an apodictic command. In these cases, the legal unit is often continued or elaborated with a כי clause, almost as if it were marking a "subcondition" rather than the main legal case.[68]

The third change is particularly important for my argument. In three cases, there is evidence of a legal structure that is distinctive of Deuteronomy, in which a new legal topos is introduced by an unconditional apodictic formulation that may be formulated in either the 2nd or the 3rd person. An example of this occurs with the law of tithes, which begins: עשר תעשר את כל תבואת זרעך ("You shall take a tenth of the entire yield of your

---

that Yahweh your God is about to give you. . . ." The second case occurs with a slight variation (use of the independent subject pronoun plus participle) in Deut 21:1. On the *Landgabeformel*, see Norbert Lohfink, "Kerygmata des deuteronomistischen Geschichtswerks," *Studien zum Deuteronomium und zur deuteronomistischen Literatur, II* (SBAB 12; Stuttgart: Katholisches Bibelwerk, 1991) 125–42. This formula, which in the first instance serves to introduce the law of the king, cannot logically mean "*If* you enter the land," at least not without calling into question the theological and narrative assumptions of the text. The NJPS renders: "If, *after* you have entered the land that the LORD your God has assigned to you" (Deut 17:14). This translation confirms the point here: the protasis marker in the land-grant formula has been rendered "after," given the contextual certainty of the fulfillment of the divine promise. The *if* represents the continuation of the protasis; it has been moved forward to simplify the construction: ואמרת (Deut 17:14b). Lohfink has demonstrated that the formula assumes the perspective of the Deuteronomistic History and reflects the incorporation of Deuteronomy into its larger historical framework (ibid., 125–42).

In other contexts, as well, the literary introduction to law in the legal corpus of Deuteronomy presupposes the larger narrative setting of the Deuteronomistic History. The commandment to make war against the autochthonous nations in order to occupy the promised land represents a divine injunction and is central to the holy war ideology of Deuteronomy (7:1–5). Thus, when the military campaign against the Canaanites serves to introduce a law, the context requires "when." There are three principal formulations: (1) כי יכרית יהוה אלהיך את הגוים, "When the Lord your God has cut down the nations" (12:29; 19:1); (2) כי תצא למלחמה על איביך, "When you go forth to battle your enemies" (20:1; 21:10); and (3) כי תצא מחנה על איביך, "When you encamp against your enemies" (23:10). A similar variation occurs in the formula כי ירחיב יהוה אלהיך את גבולך כאשר דבר לך, "*When* Yahweh your God expands your border, as he has promised you" (Deut 12:20; see also 19:8, a verbatim repetition employing אם instead of כי). The formulation stresses that the expansion of the borders represents a divine promise to the ancestors, almost certainly the patriarchs. Failure to fulfill the unconditional divine promise of the land is inconceivable, and thus the context requires "when." In fairness, the references to the ancestors in Deuteronomy are indeed a complex and unresolved scholarly issue. My position here follows Norbert Lohfink in his book-length review, *Die Väter Israels im Deuteronomium: Mit einer Stellungnahme von Thomas Römer* (OBO 111; Freiburg: Universitätsverlag / Göttingen: Vandenhoeck & Ruprecht, 1991). Lohfink here responds to the argument by Thomas Römer that these references have the exodus generation in mind. See his *Israels Väter: Untersuchungen zur Väterthematik im Deuteronomium und in der deuteronomistischen Tradition* (OBO 99; Freiburg: Universitätsverlag / Göttingen: Vandenhoeck & Ruprecht, 1990) 128 n. 53. Note also his chapter-length response in Lohfink's volume.

68. See part I of this book, pp. 25–26.

seed," 14:22a; similarly, 15:19; 19:15). Thereafter, elaborations and special applications of the original unconditional formulation may be explored by protases introduced by וכי, "but if" (Deut 14:24; similarly, 15:21), or כי, "if" (19:16). Remarkably, even though the use of כי has been expanded in the Deuteronomic legal corpus to serve as a subcondition, this expansion only holds with certainty when following an apodictic command.[69] In Deuteronomy's law code, with the possible exception of the manumission law, כי is not used in any grammatical construction to mark a subcondition of a casuistic main law marked by כי.[70] At no point in Deuteronomy, other than possibly Deut 15:16 in the manumission law (see below), is a construction involving כי used to instantiate a subcondition when following a main condition marked by כי. Just as in the Covenant Code, אם(ו) continues to function in the legal corpus of Deuteronomy to mark subconditions when they follow a casuistic main law marked by כי (Deut 22:13, 20; 22:23, 25; 24:10, 12; 25:5, 7).

In a number of cases, Deuteronomy groups sequences of separate laws in a series in which each is introduced by a conditional כי, "if" (22:6, 8; 22:22, 23, 28; 23:25, 26; 24:20, 21), but these sequences do not consist of a casuistic main law followed by a subcondition; rather, the sequences consist of a casuistic main law followed by another casuistic main law. In all such cases, the first law in the sequence has an independent protasis and a corresponding apodosis.[71] The following law will then have its own protasis

---

69. While generally agreeing that the Covenant Code adheres to a strict regulation of כי and אם and that Deuteronomy departs in its use of כי to mark a subcondition when following an apodictic formulation, Jeffrey Stackert notes a possible complication in Exod 21:14 (*Rewriting the Torah: Literary Revision in Deuteronomy and the Holiness Legislation* [FAT 52; Tübingen: Mohr Siebeck, 2007] 108 n. 204); here, in his analysis, a subcondition:

> follows a main clause formulated participially and a negatively formulated subcondition that begins with a pronominal ואשר. . . . it is possible that the author of Exodus 21:12–14 employs כי in v. 14 because, to his mind, כי must always precede אם in casuistic formulation. If this is the case, the distinction that Levinson and Zahn observe in Deuteronomy can be nuanced a bit: it is not necessarily that Deuteronomy innovates a new role for כי as marking subordinate legal conditions. Instead, because of Deuteronomy's preference for mixed legal formulations, which begin with an apodictic law that is then conditioned by casuistic, subordinate laws, these subordinate conditions can be expressed with כי if כי has not appeared previously in the legal set.

However, it is far from clear that Exod 21:12–14 represents an original compositional unit, as Stackert argues. The use of a relative clause to mark the protasis of v. 13 is anomalous within the Covenant Code.

70. There are 52 cases of protasis-marking כי in the legal corpus of Deuteronomy (chs. 12–26); see appendix 3 for a full list of occurrences.

71. Determining where the apodosis begins in Classical Hebrew is often difficult. Udo Rüterswörden builds on the investigation by Seitz (*Redaktionsgeschichtliche Studien*, 95–183).

and apodosis. This sequence may be designated כי (Law 1) + כי (Law 2). It is this type of sequence that the law of vows most resembles, rather than the conditional + subconditional sequence that Seitz and Liedke posit.

However, the law of vows remains anomalous even when compared with the sequence of כי (Law 1) + כי (Law 2). The *waw* in 23:23 distinguishes the law of vows from the other units mentioned above. Within Deuteronomy—other than in the case of the law of vows (Deut 23:22, 23)—I have not been able to find a single case with this sequence:

כי   ("if" + protasis + apodosis, marking Law 1) +
וכי   ("and/but if" + protasis + apodosis, marking Law 2)

The singularity of this case emerges more clearly when it is contrasted with the manumission law of Deuteronomy. There we have the sequence:

| 15:12 | כי ימכר לך אחיך . . . תשלחנו חפשי מעמך |
| 15:13 | וכי תשלחנו חפשי מעמך לא תשלחנו ריקם |

In this case, the structure is:

| כי + protasis + apodosis | If (new law) A . . . then B. . . . |
| וכי + apodosis repeated + לא: | But when you do B, you must not. . . . |

In Deut 15:13, וכי must be rendered as a temporal clause, since the completion of the action described in the apodosis of the previous law is now the point of departure: "*But when* you set him free, you must not send him forth empty-handed." The Hebrew idiom—or the distinction between

He seeks to provide a comprehensive analysis of the criteria for distinguishing where an apodosis begins in the legal material of Deuteronomy. He is one of few to recognize the difficulty of doing so and to emphasize correctly that no single mechanical principle operates across the board ("Die Apodosis in den Rechtssätzen des Deuteronomiums," 124–37). Although Rüterswörden provides an analysis of Deut 23:22, he discusses only the single verse and not the law as a whole (Deut 23:22–24). The focus of the discussion is only to recognize that here the apodosis is marked by the prohibition (the negative + *yiqtol*; ibid., 128). Beat Huwyler ("'Wenn Gott mit mir ist . . .' (Gen 28,20–22): Zum sprachlichen und theologischen Problem des hebräischen Konditionalsatzes," *TZ* 57 [2001] 10–25) also deals with the difficulties in determining how to recognize the transition from protasis to apodosis in a conditional sentence, when the apodosis is not formally marked, in "'Wenn Gott mit mir ist . . .' (Gen 28,20–22)," 10–25; and Raju D Kunjummen, "The Syntax of Conditionals in Deuteronomy and Translation of *wqatal* [*sic*] (Consecutive Conditionals)," http://www.biblicallaw.net/2008/kunjummen.pdf (accessed 30 August 2011). Although Kunjummen correctly recognizes that *wĕqatal* clauses do not always mark an apodosis when following a conditional clause, his argument that certain *wĕqatal* clauses represent the continuation of the preceding protasis is not convincing.

temporal and conditional in the case of כי clauses—is not lexically instantiated (marked); the distinction is purely semantic, not grammatical.[72] The
distinction turns on the understanding of the relation of the adverbial
complement to the main clause. כי clauses can function adverbially to mark
either conditional or temporal clauses. If there is an adverbial clause in
the main clause, then this clearly triggers a temporal function. In Classical
Hebrew, a narrative marker sets the context for the temporal clause. In
the Deuteronomic legal context, the narrative marker (the reference to
the conquest of the land as ex post facto future reference, for example)
commits the law to an overall narrative frame into which the particular
statement is embedded. The particle כי in this context could not plausibly
be rendered *if*, since the narrative is given.[73]

Even though the continuation elaborates the action and seeks to
refine and expand it, much as a subcondition would, וכי cannot, in this
case, mark a protasis or conditional "if."[74] In contrast, in the law of vows,
we have:

23:22	כי תדר נדר . . .
23:23	וכי תחדל לנדר . . .

Here the semantic structure is very different:

כי + protasis + apodosis:	If (new law) A . . . then B. . . .
וכי + neg. protasis + לא neg. apodosis:	But if non-A . . . then non-B. . . .

When the syntax and grammar of the law of vows is read in the context of
the rest of Deuteronomy's legal material, it becomes evident that וכי marks
neither a subcondition nor a temporal clause; there is simply no precedent
for this particular grammatical construction and syntactical relationship
between clauses that might make sense of Deut 23:23 as a subcondition.

---

72. The following draws on personal communication with Prof. George Sheets (University of Minnesota). For an analysis of conditionals from the vantage point of linguistics, see Barbara Dancygier, *Conditionals and Prediction: Time, Knowledge, and Causation
in Conditional Constructions* (Cambridge Studies in Linguistics 87; Cambridge: Cambridge
University Press, 1999).

73. The same construction, if given a different focus or context, could very conceivably
function as a true conditional. Something that is temporally contingent may also be causally
contingent; consequently, there may be some similarity between the two semantic ranges
(temporal/conditional clauses). Since Hebrew can employ the same conjunction or comple-
mentizer in both cases in legal contexts, *when* is particularly broad in its semantic range.

74. Deut 15:16 might be read as a subcondition, although its construction is anomalous
(והיה כי). This particular construction also lends itself to being read as marking a new law. In
either case, its anomalous structure does not allow for any clear parallel with Deut 23:23's וכי.

On the contrary, it does not presuppose the fulfillment of the terms of
the previous law and refine them (as with the manumission law); rather,
it marks the protasis ("if" clause) of a new law that is antithetical to the
immediately preceding law. This formulation is irregular both syntactically
(no other law in Deuteronomy uses the sequence conditional כי + subcondition וכי) and semantically (in no other sequence of two laws does the second law negate both the protasis and the apodosis of the preceding law).[75]

From two mutually independent points of view, therefore, Deut 23:23
emerges as problematic: first, it interrupts the logical connection of the
content of vv. 22 and 24; second, it creates a sequence of conditionals
not attested elsewhere in Deuteronomy's legal corpus. The incongruous
and intrusive protasis-marking כי in v. 23 is most plausibly explained as an
interpolation.

As we have seen, later interpreters found it difficult to navigate the law
precisely because the interpolation resulted in an anomalous syntactical
formulation. In order to date the interpolation, I shall now turn to the
reception of Deuteronomy's law of vows in Numbers 30.

VI. Reworking and Expansion of
Deuteronomy's Law of Vows in Numbers 30

The Priestly source has its own extensive treatment of vows in Numbers 30.[76] The focus here, however, is less on vows than on gender rela-
tions: the unit significantly restricts the independent legal status of women.
It grants women's fathers or husbands the right to annul and revoke their
vows and oaths on condition that the male takes prompt action. Only wid-
ows or divorcées (that is, women who do not live under the legal aegis of
father or husband) are treated as independent legal and religious persons
whose vows and oaths cannot be subject to revocation—as long as the vow
or oath is sworn after the death of or divorce from the husband.

---

75. The affirmation "However, there shall be no needy among you" (Deut 15:4) is
reversed by "If there is a needy person among you" (15:7). This structure helps strengthen
the hypothesis proposed here. The unit denying the existence of poverty (15:4–6) makes
little sense in context and must represent an interpolation. The entire unit is concerned with
social-welfare legislation: economic hardship is the rationale for the legislation governing
remission of debts (15:1–3). This same theme is continued in the legislation that urges lend-
ing as a response to poverty, even when the lender is faced with the near-certain loss of the
amount of the loan as the remission (seventh) year approaches (15:7–11).

76. Recent studies include Horst Seebass, *Numeri: Kapitel 22,2–36,13* (BKAT 4/3;
Neukirchen-Vluyn: Neukirchener Verlag, 2007); Reinhard Achenbach, *Die Vollendung der
Tora: Studien zur Redaktionsgeschichte des Numeribuches im Kontext von Hexateuch und
Pentateuch* (BZAR 3; Wiesbaden: Harrassowitz, 2003); and Baruch A. Levine, *Numbers 21–36*
(AB 4A; New York: Doubleday, 2000).

Baruch Levine suggests: "Another way of looking at Numbers 30 is as a reaction against what may have been the greater freedom afforded women to own property and to engage in business transactions during the Achaemenid period."[77] Levine demonstrates that the chapter's special terminology for "binding agreement" (*'esār*, also written *'issār*; pl., *'esārîm*) connects it very closely to the technical legal vocabulary of the fourth-century B.C.E. Aramaic legal papyri from Elephantine and Wadi ed-Daliyeh.[78] He demonstrates how innovative Numbers 30 is in restricting the traditional rights of women to make oaths and vows. He also shows how this unit marks an important chapter in the history of the shift from orality to literacy: "Against the background of earlier biblical references to the vow (Hebrew *neder*), what is most novel about this legislation of Numbers 30:2–17 is the pairing of the *'esār*, usually realized as a written document, with a predominantly oral or verbal legal act, the pronouncement of a vow."[79] When the two perspectives are integrated, the previously inviolable oral commitments and speech acts of women become subordinated to the superior legal power of men, who control the written instruments of law.

Another aspect of Numbers 30 strengthens Levine's hypothesis and contributes to our analysis. Part of the innovative force of the chapter is the way that it reworks and significantly expands the law of vows in Deuteronomy. The Deuteronomic law contemplated gender equality: there are no separate provisions for male and female. Indeed, just a few verses beforehand, Deuteronomy 23 treats the earnings of male and female cult prostitutes on equal terms, prohibiting both from being used in payment of vows at the temple (Deut 23:19). In fact, as fig. 2.8 demonstrates, the treatment of vows in Numbers 30 draws on our passage at a number of critical points. The general statement of vowing in Num 30:3 is patterned directly on the law of vows in Deut 23:22. It modifies the protasis marker כי into the format used by the Priestly source, איש כי, which in turn reflects the formula used in the Neo-Babylonian laws, *awīlu ša*, "a man who. . . ." After the initial part of the protasis referring to the oral swearing of the vow, Numbers continues with its elaboration: "or takes an oath to obligate himself by a binding agreement" (Num 30:3).[80]

---

77. Levine, *Numbers 21–36*, 436.

78. Ibid., 52. Levine assigns Numbers 30 its own date while regarding P more broadly as early postexilic. Achenbach argues that Numbers is a post-Priestly document and dates the book's final redaction to the early fourth century B.C.E. (*Die Vollendung der Tora*, 443–556, 557–628).

79. Levine, *Numbers 21–36*, 52.

80. For the translation, see ibid., 426.

Deuteronomy's Law of Vows (Deuteronomy 23)		Priestly Restrictions on Vows and Oaths by Women (Numbers 30)	
כי תדר נדר ליהוה אלהיך	22	איש כי ידר נדר ליהוה או השבע שבעה לאסר אסר על נפשו	3
לא תאחר לשלמו . . .		לא יחל דברו	
וכי תחדל לנדר לא יהיה בך חטא	23	[not represented]	
מוצא שפתיך תשמר ועשית	24	ככל היצא מפיו יעשה	
22	*If you make a vow to Yahweh* your God, you must *not* delay in fulfilling it. . . .	3	*If* a man *makes a vow to Yahweh* or takes an oath imposing an obligation on himself, he shall *not* break his pledge.
23	But if you refrain from vowing, it will not count against you as a sin.		[not represented]
24	*What has gone forth from your lips* you must take heed *to perform.*		According to all *that has gone forth from his mouth he shall perform.* (NJPS, modified)
Analysis (Deuteronomy 23)		Analysis (Numbers 30)	
22	*General admonition to fulfill vows*	3	*General admonition to fulfill vows,* oaths, and binding agreements
23	**Consideration of not vowing**		[not represented]
24	*What has gone forth from your lips* you must take heed *to perform*		According to all *that has gone forth from his mouth he shall perform.*

FIGURE 2.8. Priestly Reworking and Expansion of
Deuteronomy's Law of Vows (Numbers 30)

The assertion that the oath or vow should not become profaned, the apodosis, also appears to adapt its model in Deuteronomy, as does the admonition that one must perform all that issues forth from one's mouth. Most striking here is that the preliminary statement in Num 30:3 functions as a précis of the entire law of vows in Deuteronomy. It includes both the admonition to fulfill vows (Deut 23:22) and the parenesis to perform what issues forth from the mouth (Deut 23:24).[81]

The only part of the Deuteronomic law *not* to be reflected in the Numbers restatement is precisely the portion that I have proposed represents an interpolation (Deut 23:23). One can always imagine that an omission might be by design, if the omitted material is not relevant to the aims of the writer. In this case, however, an intentional omission makes little sense in the context of a chapter designed to advance the right of the husband or father to annul the vow or oath of his wife or daughter. A textual precedent promoting abstention from vows altogether (as in Deut 23:23) might well have been pressed to advantage, had it been available and known. It could have provided an additional means for the men involved to restrict the piety and autonomy of the women in their homes. The absence in Numbers 30 of any notion that simply refraining from vows is a legitimate course of action is therefore striking. It suggests, at least as a

---

81. Ibid., 440. While the author of Numbers reworked Deuteronomy's law of vows, Numbers 30 was itself the object of reworking in the *The Damascus Document* and 4QInstruction/Sapiential Work A[b] (4Q416). The *Damascus Document* qualifies the law by restricting the scope of the husband's power to annul an oath and emphasizes that a husband may annul the vows or oaths of his wife only if they would transgress the covenant; otherwise they should stand (CD 16:10–12/4Q271 4 ii 10–12; Baumgarten, *Damascus Document*, 180). See also Charlotte Hempel, *The Damascus Texts* (Sheffield: Sheffield Academic Press, 2000); and eadem, *The Laws of the Damascus Document: Sources, Tradition and Redaction* (STDJ 29; Leiden: Brill, 1998).

Whereas the *Damascus Document* restricts the husband's right to anul oaths, 4QInstruction/Sapiential Work A[b] (4Q416), a sapiential text from Qumran, interprets Numbers 30 and instead suggests that the 2nd-person addressee, the maven or husband, may annul every vow or oath made by his wife merely "by the utterance of your lips" or "mouth." The critical edition notes that "the presence in a sapiential context of this legal material on the annulment of vows is surprising; note how it has been converted from casuistic law in the 3rd sg. into 2nd sg. moral exhortations, presumably addressed in this document to the maven" (J. Strugnell et al., *Sapiential Texts, Part 2: Cave 4.XXIV* [DJD 34; Oxford: Clarendon, 1999] 123–25, 129–31 [at p. 129]). "While not a correction of Numbers 30," 4QInstruction "expresses a different stress; the material is no longer legal but has been made into an anthropological statement . . . justifying the subordination of the wife to her husband's control" (ibid., 129). DJD does not note that the change from the 3rd person of Numbers 30 to the 2nd person in 4QInstruction may indicate a use of Deut 23:24. In Deuteronomy 23, the 2nd-person addressee is the one who vows by an utterance of "your mouth" and is commanded to fulfill what goes forth from "your lips." If Numbers 30 uses Deut 23:22, 24, as I am arguing, but has changed the 2nd person to 3rd person, then perhaps the author of 4QInstruction is in some sense restoring the 2nd person of Deuteronomy 23, although the one now addressed in the 2nd person is the one who does the annulling. Also overlooking 4QInstruction's reworking of Deuteronomy 23 is Lawrence H. Schiffman, "Halakhic Elements in 4QInstruction," *Qumran and Jerusalem: Studies in the Dead Sea Scrolls and the History of Judaism* (Studies in the Dead Sea Scrolls and Related Literature; Grand Rapids, MI: Eerdmans, 2010) 204–15.

possibility, that Deut 23:23 was not known to the author of Numbers 30, even as he used elements of both Deut 23:22 and 24 as the foundation for his own systematic treatment of vows.

If we accept that Numbers 30 builds on the law of vows in Deuteronomy, while witnessing it in a form prior to the interpolation, then we have a clear *terminus a quo* of around 450 B.C.E., which is the likely date proposed for this later redactional layer in Numbers. Then, the *terminus ad quem* would be around 300 B.C.E., since the present form of the text is presupposed by both the Septuagint translator and by Qoheleth.

VII. Conclusion

The law of vows in Deut 23:22–24 is difficult both in its syntax and in the sequence of its legal content. Verse 23 represents the point of difficulty, because it both disrupts the logical sequence of the law and is syntactically anomalous. The various exegetical responses to the law in the history of interpretation suggest an implicit recognition of these problems. The divergent reformulations of the law in Qoh 5:4–7 (which rearranges the sequence of the law) and the Temple Scroll (11QT 53:11–14, which posits a formal subcondition at the point of difficulty) suggest that each of these independent witnesses sensed the textual difficulty and sought to compensate for it. *Sipre Deuteronomy* struggles in its own way with Deuteronomy's law of vows. The implicit recognition of the textual difficulties has continued into more recent times as modern biblical scholars such as Seitz and Liedke have wrestled with the syntax and sequence of the law.

The disorder that the history of interpretation reveals is best explained as the result of an interpolation. The interpolator sought to provide a correction to tradition by discouraging vowing. He created a nearly mirror opposite of the practice he opposed, even using its classical conditional. The correction addressing the older religious norm most likely originated as an interlinear comment in the manuscript. The correction of tradition imitated the formulation of the original law but reversed it, employing the negative. In the process of the transmission and copying of the manuscript, the annotation became integrated into the text.[82] At that point, it

---

82. David M. Carr provides extensive documentation for scribal revision, expansion, and adaptation in the process of teaching and transmitting the biblical text (*The Formation of the Hebrew Bible: A New Reconstruction* [New York: Oxford University Press, 2011] 37–149). His data provide a counterbalance to Emanuel Tov's valuable methodological caution ("Glosses, Interpolations, and Other Types of Scribal Additions in the Text of the Hebrew Bible," *The Greek and Hebrew Bible: Collected Essays on the Septuagint* [VTSup 72; Leiden: Brill, 1999] 53–74).

then disrupted the standard legal syntax of Deuteronomy, creating the anomalous sequence of two consecutive conditional כיs. The law would then have been difficult to read because its instantiation does not cohere with any other examples in the legal corpus of Deuteronomy. There were ancient readers who struggled with the text and decided to read it as a subcondition; and there were those who read the final construction of the unit as consisting of two independent laws.

An additional question is: why would the interpolation have been made in the first place? Circumspection about vowing was characteristic of many segments of Second Temple Judaism, as we see in a wide variety of texts and literary genres, and it shows up still later in the earliest rabbinic commentary on Deuteronomy, *Sipre Deuteronomy*. During the process of the transmission of the legal corpus of Deuteronomy in the late Second Temple period, some of the widespread debates about the wisdom of religious vows was read back into the Pentateuch. The goal was to introduce the caution against vows directly into the textual tradition of the Torah.

The response of Numbers 30 to Deuteronomy's law of vows indicates that Deuteronomy did not yet contain the disruptive verse (v. 23) when Numbers 30 was composed. This not only strengthens the case for an interpolation but dates it to sometime in the fifth or fourth centuries B.C.E. Once the interpolation was added and became accepted as part of the textual tradition, it created a ripple effect whereby readers have been forced to resolve the disruption in order to make sense of the text's content and syntax. The history of interpretation thus offers a window into the composition history of Deuteronomy's law of vows and leads to resolution of the textual difficulty through the recognition of a previously unnoticed interpolation.

Afterword

Since part 1 was originally published in 2002, discussion about the way that the Temple Scroll interacts with the Pentateuch has been carried forward by a number of scholars. The short compass prescribed by the new series that this monograph inaugurates, Critical Studies in the Hebrew Bible, precludes meaningfully engaging all of them, especially given the wide range of intellectual and methodological issues involved. The issues include the status of the Temple Scroll for its community (whether or not it was viewed as scriptural);[1] its status in relation to the Pentateuch (whether it was understood as an exegetical supplement to the Pentateuch

---

1. There has been a long debate about whether or not the Temple Scroll was regarded as Scripture within its community. After reviewing the issues, Sidnie White Crawford reaches an impasse: "Its status as Scripture remains at best uncertain" (*Rewriting Scripture in Second Temple Times* [Studies in the Dead Sea Scrolls and Related Literature; Grand Rapids, MI: Eerdmans, 2008] 102). In contrast, while recognizing that "most of the rewritten Scripture texts were not authoritative," Emanuel Tov maintains that "such a claim was made for the Temple Scroll, Jubilees, and 1 Enoch" ("The Authority of Early Hebrew Scripture Texts," *Journal of Reformed Theology* 5 [2011] 276–95 [esp. p. 292; emphasis original]). While I agree with his assessment that the Temple Scroll held authoritative status, Tov's criteria are not clearly and consistently presented. It would be helpful to clarify whether the primary basis for that determination is (a) the authority claim made by the author for the text as "revealed Scripture" (p. 292 n. 58); (b) its "popularity at Qumran," judged by the number of manuscripts attested (p. 293 n. 60); or (c) the "acceptance" of the composition as authoritative (p. 293). If acceptance is the key issue, then the question also needs to be asked: acceptance by whom—by the composer, by the copyist, or by a community (and if so, which one)?

Scribal practices at Qumran and, in particular, the writing of the divine name may provide a more reliable criterion for determining scriptural status. In nonbiblical texts, the community at Qumran tended either to write the Tetragrammaton in Paleo-Hebrew or to use four dots (*Tetrapuncta*) to represent it. This technique is employed in 4Q524, the earliest witness to the Temple Scroll. However: "11Q19 and 11Q20, both of which are later Herodian manuscripts, freely use the Tetragrammaton throughout. Therefore it is possible that the text was likely not considered to be 'Scripture' when it was composed but may have been accorded that status at a later time" (Lawrence H. Schiffman et al., "Temple Scroll Defining Edition [11Q19]," in *The Dead Sea Scrolls: Hebrew, Aramaic, and Greek Texts with English Translations*, vol. 7: *Temple Scroll and Related Documents* [ed. James H. Charlesworth et al.; Tübingen: Mohr Siebeck / Louisville: Westminster John Knox, 2011] 6). Even this criterion is not consistently accurate, however. In his analysis of the writing of the divine name at Qumran, Emanuel Tov lists several cases where the *Tetrapuncta* were also used in biblical manuscripts (*Textual Criticism of the Hebrew Bible* [3rd ed.; Minneapolis: Fortress, 2012] 205).

or existed independently);[2] the textual history of the Temple Scroll in relation to its sources;[3] the exegetical techniques of the Temple Scroll in relation to Second Temple and rabbinic law;[4] and the ability of the Temple
Scroll and other Second Temple compositions to provide empirical models

---

2. In the original publication of part 1 in 2002, Molly Zahn and I argued that the
composer of the Temple Scroll devoices and revoices Scripture in an effort to supersede
the Pentateuch. In a series of studies, without taking our article into account, Eckart Otto
insists on a distinction between Deuteronomy and the rest of the Torah ("Die Rechtshermeneutik der Tempelrolle [11QT^a]," *ZABR* 13 [2007] 159–75; repr. in idem, *Altorientalische
und biblische Rechtsgeschichte: Gesammelte Studien* [BZAR 8; Wiesbaden: Harassowitz, 2008]
547–63; idem, "Die Rechtshermeneutik im Pentateuch und in der Tempelrolle," in *Tora
in der Hebräischen Bibel: Studien zur Redaktionsgeschichte und synchronen Logik diachroner
Transformationen* [ed. Reinhard Achenbach, Martin Arneth, and Eckart Otto; BZAR 7;
Wiesbaden: Harrassowitz, 2007] 72–121; and idem, "Temple Scroll and Pentateuch: A
Priestly Debate about the Interpretation of the Torah," in *The Qumran Legal Texts between
the Hebrew Bible and Its Interpretation* [ed. Kristin De Troyer and Armin Lange; CBET 61;
Leuven: Peeters, 2011] 59–74). According to Otto, Deuteronomy, because it employs the
Mosaic voice, is substantially revised and revoiced in the 1st-person speech of God in the
Temple Scroll, while the rest of the Torah remains largely intact. His position is more fully
developed in the monograph of Simone Paganini, discussed below. By distinguishing the
different types of authoritative voicing in the Pentateuch, Otto has provided a more nuanced
understanding of the voicing employed in the Temple Scroll. However, he does not consider
cases where the Temple Scroll alters laws from the Covenant Code, Leviticus, or Numbers,
or where some of these laws may themselves have Mosaic voicing (as with Numbers 30, discussed below in the section on Paganini). See further Molly M. Zahn, "Review of Reinhard
Achenbach, Martin Arneth, and Eckart Otto, *Tora in der Hebräischen Bibel: Studien zur
Redaktionsgeschichte und synchronen Logik diachroner Transformationen*," *JAOS* 129 (2009)
329–30; and eadem, "Review of Eckart Otto, *Altorientalische und biblische Rechtsgeschichte:
Gesammelte Studien*," *JAOS* 132 (2012) 128–29.

3. In retrospect, in the original publication of part 1, Zahn and I did not adequately
distinguish between the availability of a finished Pentateuch as a resource for the Temple
Scroll composer, on the one hand, and the composer's direct dependence on the Masoretic
Text of the Pentateuch in its final form, on the other hand. In fact, there is a need for greater
recognition of the textual fluidity of the Pentateuch in the Second Temple period and of the
existence of multiple intermediary texts such as 4QReworked Pentateuch and the proto-
Samaritan Exodus as stages on the way to the sorts of exegetical changes that are manifest in
the Temple Scroll. We would now envision the development of the Temple Scroll as a more
complex process, although this would not affect our arguments in the specific cases analyzed
in the article. On the textual history of the Temple Scroll, see Molly M. Zahn, *Rethinking
Rewritten Scripture: Composition and Exegesis in the 4QReworked Pentateuch Manuscripts*
(STDJ 95; Leiden: Brill, 2011) 179–228; and eadem, "4QReworked Pentateuch C and the
Literary Sources of the Temple Scroll: A New (Old) Proposal," *DSD* 19 (2012) 133–58.

4. For a study of legal exegesis at Qumran from the perspective of both the history of
Jewish law and early biblical interpretation, see Alex P. Jassen, *Scripture and Law in the Dead
Sea Scrolls and Ancient Judaism* (Cambridge: Cambridge University Press, forthcoming). See
also Vered Noam, "Creative Interpretation and Integrative Interpretation in Qumran," in
*The Dead Sea Scrolls and Contemporary Culture: Proceedings of the International Conference
held at the Israel Museum, Jerusalem (July 6–8, 2008)* (ed. Adolfo D. Roitman, Lawrence H.
Schiffman, and Shani Tzoref; STDJ 93; Leiden: Brill, 2011), 363–76.

for contemporary pentateuchal theory.[5] One monograph, however, warrants particular attention, especially since it brings together both parts of the current study, the Temple Scroll's reworking of biblical law and the reception of Deuteronomy's law of vows in the Temple Scroll.

In his *Habilitation* thesis, Simone Paganini presents a major commentary on the way that the Temple Scroll interacts with Deuteronomy in cols. 48–66.[6] With its focus on these columns, the volume nicely complements several other recent monographs that examine the reuse of the Bible in specific sections of the Temple Scroll.[7] As the only monograph devoted entirely to the legal hermeneutics of the Temple Scroll in relation to biblical law, Paganini's study deserves a thorough response. The book's main contribution is that it provides all the relevant texts, notes the changes, and organizes them in sequence according to individual laws. Paganini compares the Temple Scroll (11Q19), its ostensible Hebrew source text in Deuteronomy, parallel manuscripts at Qumran, and the Septuagint version of Deuteronomy. While this assemblage of materials is helpful, it would have been ideal to consider the other major ancient versions (such as the Samaritan Pentateuch, the Peshiṭta, and the Vulgate) in this context as well. Including them would have provided a valuable methodological control to some of Paganini's arguments regarding the intentionality of the Temple Scroll author. Paganini recognizes that the Temple Scroll author could well have had a Hebrew Vorlage that differs from the MT.[8] Nevertheless, at a number of crucial points in his exegesis, Paganini makes

---

5. Here I believe a gap exists in the research. The most recent continental European work on the formation of the Pentateuch tends to develop its models without taking into account the evidence of Second Temple redactional compositions such as the Temple Scroll or the Samaritan Pentateuch. The situation is similar in the American context. David M. Carr's very productive engagement with the Temple Scroll tends to use it as model of textual fluidity and expansion in the process of transmission rather than as a resource for considering the hermeneutical issues entailed in the redaction of the Pentateuch (*The Formation of the Hebrew Bible: A New Reconstruction* [New York: Oxford University Press, 2011] 48–56). This disciplinary issue, where there remains room for the conceptual models employed in the fields of Old Testament/Hebrew Bible and Second Temple/Jewish studies to cross-fertilize each other, is something that I have been seeking to remedy. The present book is one step in this direction.

6. Simone Paganini, *"Nicht darfst du zu diesen Wörtern etwas hinzufügen": Die Rezeption des Deuteronomiums in der Tempelrolle—Sprache, Autoren und Hermeneutik* (BZAR 11; Wiesbaden: Harrassowitz, 2009).

7. C. D. Elledge, *The Statutes of the King: The Temple Scroll's Legislation on Kingship, 11Q19 LVI 12–LIX 21* (CahRB 56; Paris: Gabalda, 2004); Magnus Riska, *The Temple Scroll and the Biblical Text Traditions: A Study of Columns 2–13:9* (Publications of the Finnish Exegetical Society 81; Helsinki: Finnish Exegetical Society, 2001); and idem, *The House of the Lord: A Study of the Temple Scroll, Columns 29:3b–47:18* (Publications of the Finnish Exegetical Society 93; Helsinki: Finnish Exegetical Society / Göttingen: Vandenhoeck & Ruprecht, 2007).

8. Paganini, *Nicht darfst du*, 241, 260–62.

arguments about intentional textual change that base themselves on the
MT and overlook the evidence of the versions. This difficulty becomes
especially evident in his analysis of the reworking of the canon formula of
Deut 13:1, a passage that plays a crucial role in his overall understanding of
the Temple Scroll (see discussion below, pp. 89–90).

Paganini's monograph centers on how the author of the Temple Scroll
interacts with, transforms, and rewrites the MT of Deuteronomy, which,
Paganini maintains, is the ancient author's primary exegetical "target." He
argues that the Temple Scroll author is concerned to systematize the legislation of Deuteronomy in order to introduce a more logical order and to
correct the text of Deuteronomy.[9] The Temple Scroll author is especially
concerned with Moses as the speaker of Deuteronomy and as the authoritative mediator and the interpreter of Torah.[10] In part, Paganini accepts
the point of departure of the article that Zahn and I published, which
appears in the present volume as part I. He cites positively the sentence
that gives this volume its title: "It [*die Tempelrolle*] represents the attempt
to create a more perfect Torah."[11] That being said, Paganini narrows the
article's original conception considerably, so that the author of the Temple
Scroll is now concerned only to create a "besseres Deuteronomium."[12]
Paganini maintains that the ancient author's primary *agon* or 'struggle',
to use the term of literary theory, is with Deuteronomy alone and the
Mosaic mediation of revelation.[13] In Paganini's view, the Temple Scroll
author is concerned both to "de-Mosaicize" and to "de-textualize" the
Pentateuch.[14]

A number of logical difficulties arise from this approach. It risks be-
coming a circular and self-fulfilling argument, since the Temple Scroll's
transformations of Deuteronomy are the only ones examined, while the
incorporation, reworking, and recontextualization of material from elsewhere in the Pentateuch (such as Leviticus and Numbers) is not taken
into account. Paganini is careful to limit his study to cols. 48–66[15] and
to specify that his focus will be restricted to the Temple Scroll's rework-

---

9. Ibid., 252, 256.

10. Ibid., 283–90.

11. Ibid., 257 n. 40 (his insertion); see this volume, p. 14.

12. Ibid., 257.

13. As Paganini notes (ibid., 12 n. 60; 13 n. 62; 283 n. 164), his approach is strongly
influenced by Eckart Otto, "Die Rechtshermeneutik im Pentateuch und in der Tempelrolle,"
114–17.

14. Paganini, *Nicht darfst du*, 289: "Entmosaisierung, Entverschriftlichung."

15. There is some inconsistency in this regard. In several places, Paganini indicates
that the textual focus will be on cols. 45–66 (*Nicht darfst du*, 1, 3). Elsewhere, he specifies
cols. 48–66 (ibid., 29). The actual textual analysis begins with col. 48, with cols. 45:7–48:07
described as transitional and not being examined directly (ibid., 31).

ing of the legal corpus of Deuteronomy 12–26. This focus is implicit in
the monograph's subtitle: *Die Rezeption des Deuteronomiums in der Tempelrolle*. Although Paganini provides helpful charts to show how material from Deuteronomy is taken up and rearranged within this section of the Temple Scroll, these charts make no reference to the way that material from elsewhere in the Pentateuch becomes similarly reworked or is included in the new composition.[16] As such, the charts do not help the reader understand the composition of cols. 48–66 or the systematic reuse of scriptural sources in that section of the Temple Scroll. The focus is unilaterally on Deuteronomy.

That singleness of purpose might be fine in principle except that Paganini also makes a larger argument about how the Temple Scroll interacts with the Pentateuch as a whole. Paganini contends that the author of the Temple Scroll was narrowly focused on demoting the authority of Deuteronomy. In the rest of the Tetrateuch, where God serves directly as speaker and where Moses does not mediate, Paganini sees less evidence of or need for critical intervention by the Temple Scroll author. There are many places where this assumption skews the analysis. In his discussion of the unit concerned with clean and unclean animals in 11QTemple 48:1–7, the only texts presented are those relating to Deuteronomy 14 and its witnesses at Qumran.[17] The unit's interaction with the parallel list of dietary laws found in Leviticus 11 is noted briefly, and the Temple Scroll's equally significant interventions in and transformations of this source text are not investigated. Only thus can he maintain the somewhat one-sided thesis that: "Somit wurde der Text des Deuteronomiums in der Tempelrolle unter Rücksicht auf den Levitikus-Text korrigiert."[18] A more balanced presentation would recognize the extent to which the Temple Scroll's new presentation involved significant reworking of both biblical sources, not merely correcting one in light of the other.[19]

Several of these issues come to the fore in his own close study of the Temple Scroll's treatment of Deuteronomy's law of vows (11QTemple 53:11–14a + 54:5b–7), which is particularly relevant to my own discussion in the present volume.[20] Paganini's thesis that the Temple Scroll author is reacting specifically against the authority of Moses and the status of

---

16. Ibid., 247–54.

17. Ibid., 33–38.

18. Ibid., 34.

19. See Molly M. Zahn, *Rethinking Rewritten Scripture: Composition and Exegesis in the 4QReworked Pentateuch Manuscripts* (STDJ 95; Leiden: Brill, 2011) 198–204; and Carr, *Formation of the Hebrew Bible*, 51.

20. Paganini, *Nicht darfst du*, 90–100. In his analysis of the reworking of the law of vows, there is a minor transcription error. 11QTemple 53:11 should read תדור rather than תודר

Deuteronomy governs the textual analysis to the exclusion of other ways of understanding the literary phenomena under investigation. Although Paganini refers[21] to the article that Zahn and I published together, the actual analysis we provided is not engaged, whether by way of agreement or disagreement. The suggestions we made about the anomalous sequence of conditionals in Deut 23:22–24, the demonstration that Qoheleth introduced a similar sort of change in his reception of the law, and the proposal that there was a larger textual disturbance in the law of vows that required textual intervention by both Qoheleth and the Temple Scroll—these issues are not taken into consideration. Paganini instead proposes that the redundant formulation in 11QTemple 53:11, וכי אם, serves to give the initial conjunction an unambiguous conditional significance.[22] But, as shown in our article, the initial כי to mark the beginning of a legal protasis was already widely recognized as conventional and would not have required a gloss to clarify its meaning. Further, this combination of the two conjunctions normally means 'but rather' (without the initial copula), which would not make sense in this context (see pp. 34–35 of the present volume). Paganini's suggestion that אם was added to gloss an ambiguous form does not explain the text, because the alleged gloss creates rather than removes an ambiguity.

Paganini seems to overinterpret the changes made in the law of vows, often based on scant philological or text-critical evidence. The consequences for failing to fulfill a vow promptly are identified as a חטא, "sin," in Deut 23:22, 23. The word appears in the feminine form חטאה in 11QTemple 53:12. Paganini maintains that the Temple Scroll author consciously rejected the former term and replaced it with the latter.[23] He sees this change as being designed to diminish the severity of biblical law. Paganini posits a significant semantic difference between the allegedly more severe masculine form חטא and its allegedly less severe feminine alternative חטאה, as given in the Temple Scroll. Rather than examining how these forms are employed elsewhere in Deuteronomy or in the Temple Scroll, Paganini bases this hypothesis entirely on a lexicon article by Klaus Koch.[24] Despite his dependence on the lexicion article, Paganini misconstrues

---

(p. 90). Also the form תדור in 11QTemple 53:12 (corresponding to Deut 23:23) is not "3. Person des Imperfekts" (p. 93) but 2nd-person masculine.

21. Ibid., 92 n. 250.

22. Ibid., 92: "eine klar konditionale Bedeutung zuzuweisen."

23. Ibid., 93.

24. Klaus Koch, "חטא," in *Theologisches Wörterbuch zum Alten Testament* (ed. G. Johannes Botterweck and Helmer Ringgren; Stuttgart: Kohlhammer, 1977) 2:858–70. Cited by Paganini, *Nicht darfst du*, 93 nn. 256, 257; and subsequently in 168 nn. 557, 558.

Koch's position. Koch sought to make a lexical distinction that is different from the distinction that Paganini attributes to him. When he refers to the law of vows in Deuteronomy, Koch contrasts חטא not with חטאה (the form at issue in 11QTemple 53:1, and the focus of Paganini's analysis) but instead with a different feminine lexeme, חטאת.[25]

Equally significant, Paganini does not cite any Second Temple literature or DSS manuscripts in support of his proposal for an intentional replacement. A comprehensive lexical analysis of the literature at Qumran does not support any meaningful semantic distinction between the masculine and the feminine forms, let alone the idea that the feminine form reflects a less severe wrongdoing.[26] The feminine form elsewhere in the Temple Scroll marks a major trespass involving pollution caused by failure to maintain the integrity of the judicial system.[27]

Consideration of Qumran scribal practice would provide a simpler explanation of the change of forms being addressed by Paganini. After all, there is a general preference in the DSS for lengthened forms and plene spellings in order to achieve a more elevated style. Such "classicizing" or archaizing variations need not mark semantic change.[28] A similar preference is already evident in the same line, where בכה is used twice to render בך (11QTemple 53:12). Further evidence in support of this hypothesis is provided by *Hodayot*, the Thanksgiving Psalms scroll (1QH[a]). There, the short form חטא is never attested, while חטאה functions as the standard form and appears seven times.[29] Elsewhere, Paganini also sees intentional

---

25. "For Deuteronomy and P, however, *chēt'* (not *chaṭṭā'th!*) necessarily leads to the destruction of the one who bears it"; so Klaus Koch, "חטא," in *TDOT* 4:309–19 (on p. 315, emphasis his; in the German original, 2:865). Elsewhere, Paganini does report Koch's position accurately and refers to the distinction between חטא and חטאת (*Nicht darfst du*, 168–69).

26. "Die Verwendung des Nomens [חטאה] in der Tempelrolle hingegen lässt kaum eine semantische Differenz zu חטא erkennen." See Russell Fuller and Barbara Schlenke, "חטא," in *Theologisches Wörterbuch zu den Qumrantexten* (Stuttgart: Kohlhammer, 2011) 1:943–50 (on p. 948; brackets mark my addition).

27. Taking bribes, for example, causes "great guilt, thus making impure the (court) house by the iniquity of sin [חטאה]" (11Q19 51:14–15). See Lawrence H. Schiffman et al., "Temple Scroll Defining Edition (11Q19)," in *The Dead Sea Scrolls: Hebrew, Aramaic, and Greek Texts with English Translations*, vol 7: *Temple Scroll and Related Documents* (ed. James H. Charlesworth et al.; Tübingen: Mohr Siebeck / Louisville: Westminster John Knox, 2011) 126–27.

28. Steven E. Fassberg, "The Preference for Lengthened Forms in Qumran Hebrew," *Meghillot: Studies in the Dead Sea Scrolls* 1 (2003) 227–40 [Hebrew; English abstract].

29. 1QH[a] 4:24; 5:32; 9:24; 9:27; 14:9; 19:23; and 22:33. See Hartmut Stegemann, Eileen Schuller, and Carol Newsom, *1QHodayot[a], with Incorporation of 1QHodayot[b] and 4QHodayot[a–f]* (DJD 40; Oxford: Clarendon, 2009) 345. I am grateful for the assistance provided by Dr. Ingo Kottsieper and the Qumran Lexicon, Göttingen Academy of Sciences (personal e-mail, November 4, 2012).

lexical replacement operating in regard to the use of חטא, where scribal practices and syntactical smoothing would more simply explain the textual evidence.[30]

Whether Paganini regards the Temple Scroll author as taking a more severe or less severe stance toward the laws of Deuteronomy becomes unclear as his analysis proceeds. He notes the contrast between the two forms of the protasis of the law of vows:

כי תדר נדר ליהוה אלהיך לא תאחר לשלמו

If you make a vow *to Yahweh your God*, you must not delay to fulfill it. (Deut 23:22)

וכי אם תדור נדר לוא תאחר לשלמו

And if you make a vow, do not delay to fulfill it. (11QTemple 53:11)

He recognizes the omission, conventionally understood as a necessary change of syntax in order to maintain the literary fiction of the Temple Scroll, whereby Yahweh himself becomes the theonymous speaker of the text. Paganini argues against this analysis and regards the change as part of the Temple Scroll author's reworking of biblical law. Now, however, he argues that the goal of the author is to provide a significant sharpening and generalization compared with the biblical text, addressing all forms of vowing, even those not made to God.[31] It would have been helpful if Paganini had proposed an alternative way that the text might have been written, once the speaker of the text is shifted from Moses to God.[32] Paganini here also introduces an inconsistency into his analysis that is left unexplained. He represents the Temple Scroll as more lenient than its biblical source in Deut 23:22 in one case but more stringent in another case.[33]

---

30. The witness law of MT Deut 19:15 seems to contain a dittography or double reading: ולכל חטאת בכל חטא. The redundancy is removed in 11Q19 61:6: ולכל חטא. Paganini offers a convoluted explanation for this change. The Temple Scroll author allegedly replaced the first חטאת with חטא and then removed the second חטא to avoid the redundancy *(Nicht darfst du*, 168–69). The argument is circular and does not examine versional evidence meaningfully. Paganini overlooks the fact that the SP, for example, witnesses the redundancy but levels the two different terms to a consistent חטא (for the text, see Abraham Tal and Moshe Florentin, *The Pentateuch: The Samaritan Version and the Masoretic Version* [Tel Aviv: Haim Rubin Tel Aviv University Press, 2010] 577). A process of syntactical smoothing to eliminate the redundancy provides a more adequate explanation of the reading in the Temple Scroll. See Yigael Yadin, *The Temple Scroll* (3 vols.; Jerusalem: Israel Exploration Society, 1977–83) 2:178 (also noted by Paganini).

31. Paganini, *Nicht darfst du*, 94: "viel härtere und gleichzeitig allgemeinere Vorschrift zum Ausdruck zu bringen."

32. Ibid., 93.

33. Ibid., 93 and 94.

Paganini concludes his analysis of the treatment of vows in the Temple Scroll (53:11–14a), with a study of the way that it reworks the "canon formula" of Deut 13:1, the next subject that is taken up in the Temple Scroll (54:5b–7). Here Paganini develops his most distinctive argument for the hermeneutics of the Temple Scroll in relation to the Pentateuch. The source text in the MT reads: את כל הדבר אשר אנכי מצוה אתכם אתו תשמרו לעשות לא תסף עליו ולא תגרע ממנו, "The entire word that I command you shall you take care to perform; you must neither add to it nor take away from it" (Deut 13:1[12:32]). Paganini examines this verse's reflection in 11QTemple 54:5b–7, taking into account the tiny fragment 1QDeutᵃ, frg. 7 (which retains just the infinitive) and the Septuagint rendering of the verse.[34] The MT is characterized by the phenomenon of the *Numeruswechsel*, which occurs frequently in Deuteronomy, whereby the addressee shifts for no apparent reason between singular and plural. In this case, the shift takes place from 2nd-person plural (in Deut 13:1a) to 2nd-person singular (Deut 13:1b). Accurately noting that the plural addressee of MT Deut 13:1a appears in the Temple Scroll in the 2nd-person singular (כול הדברים אשר אנכי מצוכה היום), Paganini contends that this is an ideological change. He maintains that the Temple Scroll author has intentionally shifted the addressee of the text from the nation (in the plural) to Moses (in the singular). God, as speaker of the text, here allegedly chastises Moses for his tendentious transformation of the Covenant Code in the book of Deuteronomy and seeks to undercut his authority.[35]

This claim that the Temple Scroll's reworking of the canon formula is concerned to repudiate and subvert the authority of Moses becomes foundational to Paganini's entire approach. The citation that provides the title of his book, *Nicht darfst du zu diesen Wörtern etwas hinzufügen*, alludes to this reworking of the canon formula. The argument returns repeatedly within the book as a leitmotiv.[36] This claim, important as it is for his work, goes beyond the evidence. It would have been helpful for Paganini to explore how the ancient textual versions respond to the change in the grammatical number of the verse's addressee. Although he adduces the Septuagint of the verse, he overlooks the fact that the same leveling to a consistent 2nd-person singular takes place there (where Moses still remains the speaker). The corresponding change also occurs in the Samaritan Pentateuch, the Syriac, and the Vulgate.[37] Paganini's argument for an

34. Ibid., 97–99.

35. Ibid., 97: "einer sehr harten und einmaligen Aussage."

36. Ibid., 280, 288, 299, and 301.

37. See Molly M. Zahn, "Review of Simone Paganini, '*Nicht darfst du zu diesen Wörtern etwas hinzufügen*,'" *JHS* 10 (2010) 3. For more on the phenomenon of the leveling

intentional polemical rewriting of Deut 13:1 by the Temple Scroll author to serve an ideological program loses much of its force once one recognizes that the same leveling to a consistent singular is evident in the other textual witnesses as well. The reading with the singular addressee could easily have been found already in the author's Hebrew *Vorlage*, which need not have been identical to the MT. Based on the evidence of the versions, there is little reason to believe that the reading marks an intentional ideological transformation designed to demote the status of Moses.

Paganini's claim that the Temple Scroll author is concerned to de-Mosaicize Deuteronomy is an example of circular reasoning. Directly relevant evidence that might complicate or nuance the hypothesis is not considered. Paganini's stated goal is to examine the way that texts from Deuteronomy were reworked in the Temple Scroll. In principle, this would be fine and could itself provide a valuable study. But Paganini then introduces a logical and methodological inconsistency. He insists that the Temple Scroll author treated Deuteromy differently from other legal material in the Pentateuch, seeking to undermine the authority of Deuteronomy and of Moses as its speaker. This approach amounts to trying to have it both ways. Paganini's comparative argument (that the Temple Scroll author targeted Deuteronomy differently from other legal material in the Pentateuch) logically requires a comparative investigation of the way that all pentateuchal legal material is reworked in cols. 48–66 of the Temple Scroll. By restricting his analysis to the reworking of material from the legal corpus of Deuteronomy while excluding laws in Exodus, Leviticus, and Numbers that are reworked in that same textual unit, Paganini's comparative conclusions go beyond the limited textual base that he provides in support of his argument.

The Temple Scroll author does not simply resystematize the laws of Deuteronomy but rewrites and reorganizes other non-Deuteronomic legislation as well. As Zahn and I argue, the Temple Scroll author seeks to improve the editing of the Pentateuch as a whole, reordering it to bring together laws that have similar content. The Temple Scroll's treatment of the law of vows, the focus of part 2 of this volume, offers a good example (see fig. 3.1). Here the Temple Scroll author is not simply responding to Deuteronomy, in isolation from the rest of the Pentateuch, but to the redacted nature of the Pentateuch itself. The goal is to create a more logically arranged Torah. The same issue obtains in regard to the matter

---

of Deut 13:1 in the LXX and 11QTemple, see my article "The Neo-Assyrian Origins of the Canon Formula in Deuteronomy 13:1," in *Scriptural Exegesis: The Shapes of Culture and the Religious Imagination (Essays in Honour of Michael Fishbane)* (ed. Deborah A. Green and Laura Lieber; Oxford: Oxford University Press, 2009) 25–45 (at p. 36).

11Q19	53:9–10	=	Deut 12:26
	53:11–13a	=	Deut 23:22–24
	53:14b–54:5a	=	Num 30:3–16
	54:5b–55:14	=	Deuteronomy 13

FIGURE 3.1. Temple Scroll Unit on
Vows (Simplified)

of the voicing of the Torah. The Temple Scroll author does not target Deuteronomy alone in rejecting Mosaic mediation, as Paganini implies. The Temple Scroll author systematically rewrites the vows material from Numbers 30, just as he did for his Deuteronomic sources, to give it a direct divine voicing:

אִישׁ כִּי יִדֹּר נֶדֶר לַיהוה

If a man makes a vow *to Yahweh* (MT Num 30:3)

וְאִישׁ כִּי יִדֹּר נֶדֶר לִי

And if a man makes a vow to *me* (11QTemple 53:14)

The corresponding change to 1st person also takes place in 11QTemple 53:14 (revising Num 30:4) and in 11QTemple 54:21 (revising Num 30:13b). In this case, it is clear that the author of the Temple Scroll treats the Priestly unit on annulling women's vows and oaths, which is also voiced as a Mosaic address (per the superscriptions of Num 30:1–2), no differently from the vows unit of Deuteronomy.

Paganini's analysis of the Temple Scroll finally emerges as self-contradictory. On the one hand, he presents the Temple Scroll as a sharp reaction against the authority of Deuteronomy: as a "Gegendeuteronomium" or an "anti-Deuteronomium."[38] But then on the very next page, he maintains the opposite: "Die Tempelrolle hebt das Deuteronomium nicht definitiv auf, sondern korrigiert es, weitet es aus und systematisiert es."[39] The two contrasting positions are not integrated. In his conclusions, he argues that the Temple Scroll presents God as the divine exegete of his own earlier Pentateuch.[40] This approach does not do justice to the complexity

---

38. Paganini, *Nicht darfst du*, 277, 298, 299.

39. Ibid., 300.

40. Ibid., 299: "die Tempelrolle, indem sie Gott selbst als Ausleger seiner eigenen Gesetze präsentiert."

of the text. The Temple Scroll never presents itself in exegetical terms.[41] It never presents itself as a derivative gloss to a prior lemma but, rather, as an immediate divine revelation spoken by God at Sinai. While Paganini recognizes this issue, he has not found a model to articulate the hermeneutical richness of the Temple Scroll: both its implicit exegetical reworking of the Pentateuch and its explicit self-presentation as a direct divine revelation.

Within biblical studies, where there are so many competing models for understanding the formation of the Pentateuch, the Temple Scroll would seem to offer valuable empirical evidence, not only for the way that scribes worked with texts in antiquity, but for the hermeneutical issues they confronted in seeking to integrate originally inconsistent sources into a unified document. In many ways, the issues raised nearly a quarter century ago by Steven Kaufman's trenchant article, "The Temple Scroll and Higher Criticism," still have not been fully investigated.[42] The copula "and" in his title actually marks a disconnection between the two subfields; or at least it points forward to where new work remains to be done. The categories of "Scripture" and "Rewritten Scripture" are not so far apart as is often assumed. The fields of "Bible" and "Second Temple / Dead Sea Scrolls" should ideally be more closely integrated than they are today, with scholars in each subdiscipline drawing more closely on one another's work and considering each other's intellectual models. As argued in this volume, it is helpful to see the extent to which the literature of the Second Temple period often responds (in both language and content) to hermeneutical issues in the Pentateuch that result from the redactional combination of its diverse literary sources into a single Torah.[43]

As a result, there are many cases in which the phenomenon of rewritten Scripture provides a powerful way of understanding the process of composition of the Bible across a range of its genres. Even the phenomenon of regrouping or "re-redacting" specific series of laws to create a more topically coherent text, a phenomenon that is usually considered distinctive of the Temple Scroll (see pp. 14–15 and pp. 41–43 above), can be observed in very similar terms within the Pentateuch itself. The utopian combination of sabbatical, debt-release, and manumission legisla-

---

41. As noted by Karin Finsterbusch, "Review of Simone Paganini, *'Nicht darfst du zu diesen Wörtern etwas hinzufügen*,'" *TLZ* 135 (2010) 1101–3.

42. Steven A. Kaufman, "The Temple Scroll and Higher Criticism," *HUCA* 53 (1982) 29–43.

43. See Michael Bartos and Bernard M. Levinson, "'This Is the Manner of the Remission': Implicit Legal Exegesis in 11QMelchizedek as a Response to the Formation of the Torah," *JBL* 132 (2013) 351–71.

tion in Leviticus 25 arguably draws on earlier legal material found in both the Covenant Code and Deuteronomy to create a new, more integrated synthesis.[44] Similar perspectives help account for the composition of texts such as Exodus 13 and Exodus 34.[45] Here too rewritten Scripture provides biblical studies with a methodological tool to recognize the textual triggers for and the editorial techniques involved in regrouping and reinterpreting prior sequences of laws and presenting them from a new perspective. Moreover, rewritten Scripture provides a way of understanding the religious and hermeneutical stakes involved in the composition of such texts: the implicit recognition of halakic inconsistencies in the Torah, the desire to create a more coherent—a more perfect—Torah, and the attribution of the editorial intervention to prior religious tradition. Scripture, in other words, is in many cases already rewritten Scripture.

---

44. See my article, "The Manumission of Hermeneutics: The Slave Laws of the Pentateuch as a Challenge to Contemporary Pentateuchal Theory," in *Congress Volume: Leiden, 2004* (ed. André Lemaire; VTSup 109; Leiden: Brill, 2006) 281–324 (at pp. 319–324).

45. See Molly M. Zahn, "Reexamining Empirical Models: The Case of Exodus 13," in *Das Deuteronomium zwischen Pentateuch und deuteronomistischem Geschichtswerk* (FRLANT 206; Göttingen: Vandenhoeck & Ruprecht, 2004) 36–55; and Shimon Gesundheit, *Three Times a Year: Studies on the Festival Legislation of the Pentateuch* (FAT 82; Tübingen: Mohr Siebeck, 2012) 12–43.

Appendix 1:
The Use of כי and אם in Selected
Legal Texts from Qumran

TABLE 1.1 The Use of כי in *Miqṣat Maʿaśe ha-Torah* 4QMMT[1]
(Note: אם is unattested in 4QMMT)

Composite Text	Page	"If"	"Because," "For"	Other
B 16	48		x	
B 27	48	[?][2] reconstructed		
B 28	48		x	
B 32	50		[x] reconstructed	
B 48	50		[x] reconstructed	
B 53	52		x	
B 57	52		x	
B 59	52		x	
B 61	52		x	
B 65	54			x ("rather")
B 82	56		x	
C 5	58		x	
C 6	58		[x] reconstructed	
C 9	58		x	
C 13	58			x[3] ("when")

---

1. Hebrew text on which table is constructed is found in Elisha Qimron and John Strugnell, *Qumran Cave 4.V: Miqṣat Maʿaśe ha-Torah* (DJD 10; Oxford: Clarendon, 1994).

2. The edition's reconstruction of conditional כי here rather than the contextually more likely אשר is doubtful; see p. 11 n. 33 above.

3. Quotation from Deut 30:1–3.

TABLE I.2. The Use of כי in the *Damascus Document*[4]

Damascus Document	Page	"If"	"Because," "For"	"When"	כי אם ("Except," "Unless")	Other
266 2 i 2	34		x			
266 2 i 13 (1:8)	34		x			
266 3 ii 3 (5:15)	41				x ("unless")	
266 5 i 10	47		x			
266 5 i 18	48		x			
266 5 i c–d 2	49		x			
266 6 i 7	52		x			
266 7 i 3	61				x ("except")	
266 8 i 9 (15:17)	63		x			
266 8 ii 7 (16:22)	65		x			
266 8 iii 7 (10:8)	66		x			
266 9 i 4 (10:18)	67				x ("except")	
266 9 iii 2 (13:15)	70				x ("unless")	
266 11 7	76		x			
267 2 5 (5:21)	97		x			
267 2 13 (6:6)	98		x			
267 4 11	100		x			
267 6 1[5]	102					
267 9 v 5 (14:2)	109					x[6] ("though")
268 1 3	119		x			
268 1 10 (1:3)	119		x			
269 8 ii 4	131				x[7]	
269 9 2	132		x[8]			
270 4 4	152				x	
270 5 16	154		x			
270 6 iii 15 (16:22)	158		x			

4. Hebrew text on which table is constructed is found in Joseph M. Baumgarten, *Qumran Cave 4.XIII: Damascus Document (4Q266–273)* (DJD 18; Oxford: Clarendon, 1996).
   5. Fragmentary text.
   6. Written כי^א.
   7. Written כיא.
   8. Written כיא.

TABLE 1.2. The Use of כי in the *Damascus Document (cont.)*

Damascus Document	*Page*	*"If"*	*"Because," "For"*	*"When"*	כי אם ("Except," "Unless")	*Other*
270 6 iv 18	159		x			
270 7 i 14	163		x			
271 3 4[9]	175		x			
271 3 4	175			x		
271 3 9	175		x			
271 3 13	175				x	
271 4 ii 4 (16:2)	178		x			
271 4 ii 4 (16:2)	178		x			
271 5 i 2 (11:5)	180				x ("more than")	
272 2 3[10]	191					
273 5 2	197		x			

9. See Deut 22:5
10. Fragmentary text.

TABLE 1.3. The Use of אם in the *Damascus Document*

Damascus Document	Page	"If"	כי אם ("Except," "Unless")
266 1 20	31	x	
266 6 i 1	52	x	
266 6 i 10	52	x	
266 6 i 11	52	x	
266 6 i c 2 [II]	54		
266 6 ii 2	55	x	
266 6 ii 12	55	x	
266 6 iii 8	58	x	
266 7 i 3	61		x
266 8 i 4 (15:13)	63	x	
266 9 iii 2 (13:15)	70		x
266 10 ii 1	74	x	
266 10 ii 8 (7:11)	74	x	
267 1 2	96	x	
267 6 1	102	x	
267 6 7	103	x	
267 7 5	103	x	
269 8 ii 4	131		x
270 3 ii 16	147	x	
270 3 ii 17	147	x	
270 4 2	152	x	
270 4 4	152		x
270 5 21	154		x
270 6 ii 6 (15:13)	156	x	
270 6 iii 19 (9:5)	158		x ("only")
270 6 iii 19 (9:6)	158	x	
270 6 iv 12 (9:21)	159	x	
270 6 v 18 (11:13)	161	x	
271 2 11	173		x
271 3 7	175	x	
271 3 13	175		x
271 4 ii 7 (16:5)	178	x	
271 4 ii 11 (16:11)	178	x	

11. Fragmentary text.

TABLE I.3. The Use of אם in the *Damascus Document (cont.)*

Damascus Document	*Page*	*"If"*	כי אם ("*Except*," "*Unless*")
271 4 ii 11 (16:11)	178	x	
271 4 ii 12 (16:12)	178	x	
271 4 ii 15 (16:16)	178	x	
271 5 i 3 (11:6)	180	x	
271 5 i 4 (11:8)	180	x	
271 5 i 8 (11:13)	180	x	
271 5 i 20 (12:5)	181	x	
272 1 i 9	188	x	
273 4 ii 5 (16:11)	196	x	

TABLE 1.4. (א)כי in 1QS[12]

Text	Form	"If"	"Because," "For"	"When"	Other
2:14	כיא		x		
2:24	כיא		x		
3:2	כיא		x		
3:6	כיא		x		
4:16	כיא		x		
4:18	כיא		x		
4:19	כיא				x (relative)
4:22	כיא		x		
4:25	כיא		x		
5:11	כיא		x		
5:11 (2)	כיא		x		
5:13	כיא		x		
5:14	כי אם				x ("rather")
5:14 (2)	כיא		x		
5:15	כיא				x ("rather")
5:15 (2)	כיא		x		
5:17	כיא		x		
5:17 (2)	כיא		x		
5:19	כיא		x		
5:20	וכיא				x[13]
5:26	כיא		x		
6:4	כיא			x (והיה כיא)	
6:11	וכיא	x			
9:1	כיא		x		
10:2	כיא			x	
10:16	כיא		x		
10:18	כיא		x		
11:2	כיא				x (relative?)
11:3	כיא		x		
11:4	כיא		x		
11:10	כיא		x		
11:10 (2)	כיא		x		
11:17	כיא		x		

12. Hebrew text on which table is constructed is found in James H. Charlesworth et al., eds., *The Dead Sea Scrolls: Hebrew, Aramaic, and Greek Texts with English Translations*, vol. 1: *Rule of the Community, and Related Documents* (Princeton Theological Seminary Dead Sea Scrolls Project; Tübingen: Mohr Siebeck / Louisville: Westminster John Knox, 1994) 1–51.

13. Meaning unclear; Charlesworth translates "and therefore."

Table 1.5. אם in 1QS

Text	Form	"If"	Other
5:14	כי אם		x ("rather")
6:13	אם	x	
6:14	ואם	x	
6:18	ואם	x	
6:21	ואם	x	
6:24	אם	x	
7:1	ואם	x	
7:2	ואם	x	
7:3	ואם	x	
7:5	ואם	x	
7:6	ואם	x	
7:8	ואם	x	
7:11	ואם	x	
7:17	ואם	x	
7:19	אם	x	
7:21	ואם	x	
8:2	אם		x ("with" = עם!)
8:24	ואם	x	
8:25	אם	x	
8:26	אם	x	
11:11	אם		x ("when")
11:12	ואם		x ("when")
11:13	ואם		x ("when")

Appendix 2

TABLE 2.1. The Use of כי and the Spacing System
of the Temple Scroll

Closed   In the MT, a closed paragraph appears (סתומה); in 11QTemple, an interval appears within a line or at beginning of a line.

Open   In the MT, an open paragraph appears (פתוחה); in 11QTemple, a כי clause begins a new line, and there is an interval at the end of the previous line.

∅   In the MT, no סתומה or פתוחה appears; in 11QTemple, no interval appears (other than the normal space between words).

11QT	Form	Meaning	Space	Comment	MT	Spacing
3:6	כי אם	but rather	∅			
16:5	כי	for	∅			
17:2	כי	for	∅			
21:7	כי	for	∅			
22:15	כי	for	∅			
25:11	כי	for	∅			
27:6	כי	for	∅			
32:15	כי	for	∅			
35:13	כי	for	∅			
43:5	כי	for	∅			
43:12	כי	for	∅			
43:16	כי	for	∅			
45:7	ואיש כי	if	Closed			
45:11	ואיש כיא	if	Line-beginning	Previous line is flush left		
45:14	כי	for	∅			
47:8	כי	for/but	∅			
47:10	כי	for	∅			
47:11	כי	for/but	∅			
47:15	כי	for	∅			
48:6	כי	for	∅			
48:10	כי	for	∅			
48:12	כי אם	but rather	∅			

TABLE 2.1. The Use of כי and the Spacing System
of the Temple Scroll *(cont.)*

11QT	Form	Meaning	Space	Comment	MT	Spacing
49:5	ואדם כיא	if	Open			
50:2	כי	for	Uncertain			
50:10	ואשה כי	for	Open			
50:18	כי	for	∅			
51:7	כי	for	Closed			
51:13	כי	for	∅			
52:4	כי	for	∅			
52:5	כי	for	∅			
52:14	כי אם	but rather	∅			
52:18	כי	for	∅			
53:6	כי	for	∅			
53:11	וכי אם	if (pleonasm)	Line-beginning	Previous line is flush left		
53:11	כי	for	∅			
53:14	ואיש כי	if	Closed		Num 30:3	∅
53:16	ואשה כי	if	Closed		Num 30:4	∅
53:21	כי	for	∅			
54:11	כי	for	∅			
54:15	כי	for	∅			
56:12	כי	when	Open	Land grant formula	Deut 17:14	∅
57:16	כי אם	but rather	∅			
57:17	כי	for	∅			
58:3	והיה כי	if	Open			
58:10	וכי אם	if (pleonasm)	Line-beginning	Previous line is flush left		
60:10	כי	for	∅			
60:12	וכי	if	Closed		Deut 18:6	Closed
60:16	כי	when	Open	Land grant formula	Deut 18:9	Closed
60:19	כי	for	∅			
60:21	כי	for	Closed		Deut 18:14	Closed
61:2	וכי	if	Closed		Deut 18:21	∅
61:12	כי	if	Closed		Deut 20:1	Closed
61:14	כי	for	∅			

TABLE 2.1. The Use of כי and the Spacing System
of the Temple Scroll *(cont.)*

11QT	Form	Meaning	Space	Comment	MT	Spacing
62:5	כי	if	Closed		Deut 20:10	Closed
62:14	כי	for/but	Ø			
63:3	כי	for	Ø			
63:10	כי	if	Open	Whole line left blank	Deut 21:10	Closed
64:2	כי	if	Open		Deut 21:18	Closed
64:6	כי	if	Closed		cf. Deut 21:22	Closed
64:9	כי	if	Closed		Deut 21:22	Closed
64:11	כי	for/but	Ø			
64:11	כי	for	Ø			
65:2	כי	if	Uncertain		Deut 22:6	Open
65:5	כי	if	Closed[1]		Deut 22:8	Closed
65:6	כי	for[2]	Ø		Deut 22:8	Ø
65:7	כי	if	Closed		Deut 22:13	Closed
65:15	כי	for	Ø			
66:6	כיא	for	Ø			
66:7	כי	for	Ø			
66:8	כי	if	Closed		Deut 22:15	Closed
66:13	כי	for	Ø			
66:15	כי	for	Ø			
66:17	כי	for	Ø			

1. Reading a closed paragraph interval with Yigael Yadin, ed., *The Temple Scroll* (3 vols.; Jerusalem: Israel Exploration Society, 1977–83) 2:293; see also vol. 3 (col. 65, pl. 80). Contrast Elisha Qimron, ed., *The Temple Scroll: A Critical Edition with Extensive Reconstructions* (Beer-sheva: Ben-Gurion University of the Negev Press; Jerusalem: Israel Exploration Society, 1996) 90. Qimron does not identify a space here. Although indeed the space is not as wide as others (the space on line 7 is approximately three letters wide), this interval (about two letters wide) is distinct from the normal single-letter interval between words.

2. The translation of the particle here as a causal ("for") reflects the biblical source (MT Deut 22:8bβ). The contrary translation ("if") in both the NRSV and the NJPS is impossible, since conditional כי would occur at the beginning of a sentence, not in medial or final position. In effect, the NRSV and NJPS have constructed a legal protasis that hangs in the air without the necessary following apodosis. Since כי here introduces the final clause of the sentence, it must mark the motive clause and should be translated "for" or "because." To confirm this analysis, note how precisely the syntax of this law (Deut 22:8) corresponds to that of Deut 23:22. Their common structure consists of: (A) a protasis introduced by conditional כי + (B) an apodosis + (C) a motive clause that is introduced by causal כי and the emphatic rhetoric of which is marked by the doubling of the verbal root. (For the rule

TABLE 2.2. The Use of אם and the Spacing System of the Temple Scroll

KEY TO SYMBOLS

Closed   In the MT, a closed paragraph appears (סתומה); in 11QTemple, an interval appears within a line or at beginning of a line.

Open   In the MT, an open paragraph appears (פתוחה); in 11QTemple, a כי clause begins a new line, and there is an interval at the end of the previous line.

∅   In the MT, no סתומה or פתוחה appears; in 11QTemple, no interval appears (other than the normal space between words).

11QT	*Form*	*Meaning*	*Space*	*Comment*	*MT*	*Spacing*
3:6	כי אם	but rather	∅			
15:15	ואם	if	Open			
43:13	ואם	if	∅		Deut 14:24 has כי	∅
47:15	אם	if	∅			
47:16	ואם	if	∅			
48:12	כי אם	but rather	∅			
50:7	ואם	if	∅			
50:12–13	ואם	if	∅			
52:9	ואם יהיה	if	∅		Deut 15:21 has כי	∅
52:14	כי אם	but rather	∅			
53:11	וכי אם	if (pleonasm)	Line-beginning	Previous line flush left; see כי table		
53:12	ואם	if	∅		Deut 23:23 has כי	∅
53:19–20	ואם	if	Closed		Num 30:6	∅
54:8	אם	if	Open		Deut 13:2 has כי	Open
54:19	ואם	if	Open (TS = SP)[3]		Deut 13:7 has כי	∅

that conditional כי occurs in initial, not final position, see Anneli Aejmelaeus, "The Function and Interpretation of כי in Biblical Hebrew," *JBL* 105 [1986] 193–209; repr. in eadem, *On the Trail of [the] Septuagint Translators: Collected Essays* [Kampen, Netherlands: Kok Pharos, 1993] 166–85 [at p. 170]).

3. Both the Temple Scroll and the Samaritan Pentateuch correctly recognize that Deut 13:7 marks the beginning of a new legal paragraph. In contrast, the MT has no paragraph marker according to the manuscript of Leningrad Codex, folio 107 verso; see David Noel Freedman, ed., *The Leningrad Codex: A Facsimile Edition* (Grand Rapids, MI: Eerdmans /

TABLE 2.2. The Use of אם and the Spacing System
of the Temple Scroll *(cont.)*

11QT	Form	Meaning	Space	Comment	MT	Spacing
55:2	אם	if	Open		Deut 13:13 has כי	Closed
55:13	אם	if	Line-beginning	Previous line flush left	Deut 13:19 has כי [4]	∅
55:15	אם	if	Closed		Deut 17:2 has כי	Closed
57:16	כי אם	but rather	∅			
57:18	ואם	if	∅			
58:6	ואם	if	∅			
58:7	ואם	if	∅			
58:10	וכי אם	if (pleonasm)	Line-beginning	Previous line flush left; see כי chart		
58:11	והיה אם	if	Closed			
58:15	ואם	if	Closed		Deut 20:1 has כי	Closed
59:16	ואם	if	Closed		Lev 26:3	Closed
61:7	אם	if	∅		Deut 19:16 has כי	∅
62:6	והיה אם	if	∅			
62:8	ואם	if	∅			
64:14	ואם	if	∅			
66:4	ואם	if	∅			

Leiden: Brill, 1998) 226. Printed versions, reflecting later halakic convention, follow the definition of the unit in the SP and the Temple Scroll and insert a closed paragraph. On this contrast, see the careful edition of Aron Dotan, ed., *Biblia Hebraica Leningradensia: Prepared According to the Vocalization, Accents, and Masora of Aaron ben Moses ben Asher in the Leningrad Codex* (Peabody, MA: Hendrickson, 2001) xix, 1239.
    4. This כי cannot mark a protasis: it lacks an apodosis. Thus it is asseverative in meaning: "truly" or "indeed." See Bruce K. Waltke and M. O'Connor, *An Introduction to Biblical Hebrew Syntax* (Winona Lake, IN: Eisenbrauns, 1990) 662–65 (§39.3.4a–e); Ronald J. Williams, *Hebrew Syntax: An Outline* (3rd ed.; Toronto: Toronto University Press, 2007) §449; and Paul Joüon and Takamitsu Muraoka, *A Grammar of Biblical Hebrew* (2 vols.; SubBi 14/1–2; Rome: Pontifical Biblical Institute, 1991) 2:617–18 (§164b); 2 vols. in 1 (3rd ed.; SubBi 27; Rome: Pontifical Biblical Institute, 2006) 581.

Appendix 3

TABLE 3.1. All Laws with Protasis-Marking כי/וכי
in Deuteronomy 12–26

Deut	Topic of Law	כי *Marks Protasis*	Commentary on Context
12:20	Centralization	כי	*Land-grant formula*: "When Yahweh your God expands your boundaries, as he has promised you . . ." (cannot be "if" in context)
12:21	Centralization	כי	If
12:29	Centralization	כי	*When* Yahweh your God cuts down the nations . . .
13:2	Apostasy series	כי	
13:7	Apostasy series	כי	
13:13	Apostasy series	כי	
14:24	Tithes	וכי	Coordinated composite protasis (no apodosis until 14:25): וכי ("and if") . . . כי ("if") . . . כי ("if") . . . . כי ("because"). Note that unit began with apodictic law in 14:22.
15:7	Poverty	וכי	Note that כי in 15:8 is not conditional (not followed by imperfect) but asseverative or emphatic (introduces infinitive-absolute construction)
15:12	Manumission	כי	Protasis marker = "if"
15:13	Manumission	כי	"When" (presupposes completion of apodosis in previous verse and elaborates on it)
15:16	Manumission		והיה כי; different construction; new beginning
15:21	Firstlings	וכי	
17:2	Local justice	כי	
17:8	Central justice	כי	
17:14	Law of King	כי	When you enter the land that Yahweh your God is about to give you. . .
18:6	Levites	וכי	

TABLE 3.1. All Laws with Protasis-Marking כי/וכי
in Deuteronomy 12–26 *(cont.)*

Deut	Topic of Law	כי *Marks Protasis*	Commentary on Context
18:9	Prophecy series	כי	Slight variant of 17:14
18:21	Prophecy series	וכי	
19:1	Refuge cities series	כי	*When* Yahweh your God cuts down the nations . . .
19:11	Refuge cities series	וכי	
19:16	Witness law	כי	
20:1	War law series	כי	*When* you go forth to battle your enemies . . .
20:10	War law series	כי	
20:19	War law series	כי + כי + כי	Only initial כי is conditional; following two are "for" or "because"
21.1	Corpse discovered	כי	
21:10	Female captive	כי	*When* you go forth to battle your enemies . . .
21:15	Preferred wife	כי	
21:18	Rebellious son	כי	
21:22	Exposed corpse	וכי	
22:6	Nestling on path	כי	Separate laws; unrelated protases/apodoses
22:8	Parapet	כי	Separate laws; unrelated protases/apodoses
22:13	Dishonest bride	כי	
22:22	Marriage law	כי	Separate laws; different cases: here, adultery
22:23	Marriage law	כי	Separate law: rape of betrothed virgin in city; note that its subconditions are logically marked with ואם (v. 25); internal כי (vv. 26, 27) = "because"
22:28	Marriage law	כי	Separate law: rape of unbetrothed virgin
23:10	War law	כי	Separate law: war law protasis = "*When* you encamp against your enemies . . ."
23:11	War law	כי	*If* there is a man among you (nocturnal emission)

TABLE 3.1. All Laws with Protasis-Marking כי/וכי
in Deuteronomy 12–26 *(cont.)*

Deut	*Topic of Law*	*כי Marks Protasis*	*Commentary on Context*
23:22	Vows	כי	
23:23	Vows	וכי	Some tertiary witnesses read כי (MSS of Sam., medieval MSS of Vg.)
23:25	Vineyard gleanings	כי	Separate laws
23:26	Standing grain	כי	Separate laws
24:1	Divorce	כי	כי . . . + . . . והיה אם + כי, "If . . . and if it should be . . . because"
24:3b	Divorce		או כי ימות, "Or should he die . . ." Complex composite protasis; no apodosis yet introduced
24:5	Bridegroom	כי	
24:7	Kidnapping	כי	
24:10	Lending	כי	
24:19	Gleanings series	כי	
24:20	Olive harvest	כי	Separate cases; distinct and independent protases
24:21	Vineyard	כי	
25:5	Inheritance	כי	
25:11	Woman intervenes	כי	
26:12	Tithes	כי	

Bibliography

Achenbach, Reinhard. *Die Vollendung der Tora: Studien zur Redaktionsgeschichte des Numeribuches im Kontext von Hexateuch und Pentateuch.* BZAR 3. Wiesbaden: Harrassowitz, 2003.

_____ , Martin Arneth, and Eckart Otto, eds. *Tora in der Hebräischen Bibel: Studien zur Redaktionsgeschichte und synchronen Logik diachroner Transformationen.* BZAR 7. Wiesbaden: Harrassowitz, 2007.

Aejmelaeus, Anneli. "The Function and Interpretation of כי in Biblical Hebrew." *JBL* 105 (1986) 193–209. Reprinted, pages 166–85 in *On the Trail of [the] Septuagint Translators: Collected Essays.* Kampen: Kok Pharos, 1993. [The 2nd rev. ed. of this volume, published by Peeters in 2007, does not include this essay.]

Allegro, John M. *Qumran Cave 4.1 (4Q158–4Q186).* DJD 5. Oxford: Clarendon, 1968.

Altshuler, David. "On the Classification of Judaic Laws in the *Antiquities* of Josephus and the Temple Scroll of Qumran." *AJSReview* 7–8 (1982–83) 1–14.

Attridge, Harold W., Torleif Elgvin, J. T. Milik, Saul Olyan, John Strugnell, Emanuel Tov, James C. VanderKam, and Sidnie White, in consultation with James C. VanderKam. *Qumran Cave 4.VIII: Parabiblical Texts, Part I.* DJD 13. Oxford: Clarendon, 1994.

Baillet, Maurice, J. T. Milik, and Roland de Vaux. *Les "petites grottes" de Qumran.* DJD 3. Oxford: Clarendon, 1962.

Bandstra, Barry L. *The Syntax of Particle כי in Hebrew and Ugaritic.* Ph.D. Dissertation, Yale University, 1982.

Bar, Tali. "Expression of Temporality, Modality, and Perfectivity in Contemporary Hebrew Conditionals as Compared with Non-Conditionals." *WZKM* 91 (2001) 49–81.

Barthélemy, Dominique, and J. T. Milik. *Qumran Cave I.* DJD 1. Oxford: Clarendon, 1955.

Barton, George Aaron. *A Critical and Exegetical Commentary on the Book of Ecclesiastes.* ICC. New York: Scribner, 1908. Reprinted, Edinburgh: T. & T. Clark, 1959.

Bartos, Michael, and Bernard M. Levinson. "'This Is the Manner of the Remission': Implicit Legal Exegesis in 11QMelchizedek as a Response to the Formation of the Torah." *JBL* 132 (2013) 351–71.

Barzilai, Gaby. "Women's Vows," http://www.biu.ac.il/JH/Parasha/eng/matot/bar1.html [accessed 17 December 2012].

Baumgarten, Joseph M. *Qumran Cave 4.XIII: The Damascus Document (4Q266–273).* DJD 18. Oxford: Clarendon, 1996.

Bendavid, Abba. *Biblical Hebrew and Mishnaic Hebrew.* 2 vols. Tel Aviv: Dvir, 1967–71. [Hebrew]

Benigni, Antonella. "The Biblical Hebrew Particle כִּי from a Discourse Analysis Perspective." *ZAH* 12 (1999)126–45.

Benoit, Pierre J., J. T. Milik, and Roland de Vaux. *Les grottes de Murabbaʿat.* DJD 2. Oxford: Clarendon, 1961.

Berlinerblau, Jacques. *The Vow and the "Popular Religious Groups" of Ancient Israel: A Philological and Sociological Inquiry.* JSOTSup 210. Sheffield: Sheffield Academic Press, 1996.

Bernstein, Moshe J. "Pseudepigraphy in the Qumran Scrolls: Categories and Functions." Pages 1–26 in *Pseudepigraphic Perspectives: The Apocrypha and Pseudepigrapha in Light of the Dead Sea Scrolls.* Edited by Esther G. Chazon and Michael Stone. STDJ 31. Leiden: Brill, 1999.

_____, and Shlomo A. Koyfman. "The Interpretation of Biblical Law in the Dead Sea Scrolls: Forms and Methods." Pages 61–87 in *Biblical Interpretation at Qumran.* Edited by Matthias Henze. Grand Rapids, MI: Eerdmans, 2005.

Bertholet, Alfred. *Deuteronomium.* KHC 5. Leipzig and Tübingen: Mohr, 1899.

Bottéro, Jean. *Mesopotamia: Writing, Reasoning, and the Gods.* Chicago: University of Chicago Press, 1992.

Brekelmans, Christianus. "Wisdom Influence in Deuteronomy." Pages 28–38 in *La Sagesse de l'Ancien Testament.* Edited by M. Gilbert. BETL 51. Gembloux: Duculot / Leuven: Leuven University Press, 1979. Reprinted, pages 123–34, in *A Song of Power and the Power of Song: Essays on the Book of Deuteronomy.* Edited by Duane L. Christensen. Sources for Biblical and Theological Study 3. Winona Lake, IN: Eisenbrauns, 1993.

Brin, Gershon. "The Bible as Reflected in the *Temple Scroll.*" Pages 182–224 in *Shnaton: An Annual for Biblical and Ancient Near Eastern Studies* 4. Edited by Moshe Weinfeld. Jerusalem: Israel Bible Society, 1980. [Hebrew; English abstract]

_____. "Divorce at Qumran." Pages 231–44 in *Legal Texts and Legal Issues.* Edited by Moshe J. Bernstein, Florentino García Martínez, and John Kampen. STDJ 23. Leiden: Brill, 1997.

Broshi, Magen, ed. *The Damascus Document Reconsidered.* Jerusalem: Israel Exploration Society and Shrine of the Book, Israel Museum, 1992.

Carr, David M. *The Formation of the Hebrew Bible: A New Reconstruction.* New York: Oxford University Press, 2011.

Cartledge, Tony W. *Vows in the Hebrew Bible and the Ancient Near East.* JSOTSup 147. Sheffield: Sheffield Academic Press, 1992.

Charlesworth, James H., Frank Moore Cross, Jacob Milgrom, Elisha Qimron, Lawrence H. Schiffman, Loren T. Stuckenbruck, and R. E. Whitaker. *The Dead Sea Scrolls: Hebrew, Aramaic, and Greek Texts with English Translations,* vol. 1: *Rule of the Community and Related Documents.* Princeton Theological Seminary Dead Sea Scrolls Project. Tübingen: Mohr Siebeck / Louisville: Westminster John Knox, 1994.

_____, H. W. Rietz, L. H. Schiffman, M. T. Davis, C. D. Elledge, Loren L. Johns, A. Gross, and S. Haile. *The Dead Sea Scrolls: Hebrew, Aramaic, and Greek Texts with English Translations,* vol. 7: *Temple Scroll and*

Related Documents. Princeton Theological Seminary Dead Sea Scrolls Project. Tübingen: Mohr Siebeck / Louisville: Westminster John Knox, 2011.

_____, James C. VanderKam, and Monica Brady. *Miscellaneous Texts from the Judaean Desert*. DJD 38. Oxford: Clarendon, 2000.

Chavel, Simeon. "At the Boundary of Textual and Literary Criticisms: The Case of כי in Lev 20:9." *Textus* 20 (2000) 61–70.

Chirichigno, Gregory C. *Debt-Slavery in Israel and the Ancient Near East*. JSOTSup 141. Sheffield: Sheffield Academic Press, 1993.

Claassen, Walter T. "Speaker-Oriented Functions of *Kî* in Biblical Hebrew." *JNSL* 11 (1983) 29–46.

Clines, David J. A., ed. *Dictionary of Classical Hebrew*. 8 vols. Sheffield: Sheffield Academic Press, 1993–2011.

Cohen, Chaim. "The Ugaritic Hippiatric Texts: Revised Composite Text, Translation, and Commentary." *UF* 28 (1996) 105–53.

_____, and Daniel Sivan. *The Ugaritic Hippiatric Texts: A Critical Edition*. AOS 9. New Haven, CT: American Oriental Society, 1983.

Collins, John J. "Changing Scripture." Pages 23–46 in *Changes in Scripture: Rewriting and Interpreting Authoritative Traditions in the Second Temple Period*. Edited by Hanne von Weissenberg, Juha Pakkala, and Marko Marttila. BZAW 419. Berlin: de Gruyter, 2011.

Conklin, Blane. *Oath Formulas in Biblical Hebrew*. Linguistic Studies in Ancient West Semitic 5. Winona Lake, IN: Eisenbrauns, 2011.

Crawford, Sidnie White. "Review of C. D. Elledge, *The Statutes of the King: The Temple Scroll's Legislation on Kingship (11Q19 LVI12–LIX21)*." *CBQ* 67 (2005) 682–84.

_____. *Rewriting Scripture in Second Temple Times*. Studies in the Dead Sea Scrolls and Related Literature. Grand Rapids, MI: Eerdmans, 2008.

_____. *The Temple Scroll and Related Texts*. Companion to the Qumran Scrolls 2. Sheffield: Sheffield Academic Press, 2000.

_____. "The Use of the Pentateuch in the Temple Scroll and the Damascus Document in the Second Century B.C.E." Pages 301–17 in *The Pentateuch as Torah: New Models for Understanding Its Promulgation and Acceptance*. Edited by Gary N. Knoppers and Bernard M. Levinson. Winona Lake, IN: Eisenbrauns, 2007.

Danby, Herbert. *The Mishnah*. London: Oxford University Press and Cumberledge, 1933.

Dancygier, Barbara. *Conditionals and Prediction: Time, Knowledge, and Causation in Conditional Constructions*. Cambridge Studies in Linguistics 87. Cambridge: Cambridge University Press, 1999.

Delitzsch, Franz. *Biblischer Commentar über die Poetischen Bücher des Alten Testaments*, vol. 4: *Hoheslied und Koheleth*. Biblischer Commentar über das Alte Testament. Leipzig: Dörffling and Franke, 1875. ET: *Commentary on the Song of Songs and Ecclesiastes*. Translated by M. G. Easton. Commentaries on the Old Testament. Edinburgh: T. & T. Clark, 1891. Reprinted, Grand Rapids, MI: Eerdmans, 1950.

Dotan, Aron, ed. *Biblia Hebraica Leningradensia: Prepared According to the Vocalization, Accents, and Masora of Aaron ben Moses ben Asher in the Leningrad Codex*. Peabody, MA: Hendrickson, 2001.

Driver, Samuel Rolles. *A Critical and Exegetical Commentary on Deuteronomy*. 3rd ed. ICC. Edinburgh: T. &. T. Clark, 1902.

Duling, Dennis C. "'[Do Not Swear . . .] by Jerusalem Because It Is the City of the Great King' (Matt 5:35)." *JBL* 110 (1991) 291–309.

Elledge, C. D. *The Statutes of the King: The Temple Scroll's Legislation on Kingship (11Q19 LVI12–LIX21)*. CahRB 56. Paris: Gabalda, 2004.

Elon, Menahem. *Jewish Law: History, Sources, Principles*. 4 vols. Philadelphia: Jewish Publication Society, 1994.

Elwolde, John F. "Non-Biblical Supplements to Classical Hebrew ʾIM." *VT* 40 (1990) 221–23.

Engle, John. "Review of Horst Seebass, *Numeri: Kapitel 22,2–36:13*." *RBL* 3 (2011). http://www.bookreviews.org. [accessed 25 August 2011]

Even-Shoshan, Abraham. *A New Concordance to the Bible*. 2nd ed. Jerusalem: Kiryat Sepher, 1997.

Fassberg, Steven E. "On the Syntax of Dependent Clauses in Ben Sira." Pages 56–71 in *The Hebrew of the Dead Sea Scrolls and Ben Sira*. Edited by Takamitsu Muraoka and John F. Elwolde. STDJ 26. Leiden: Brill, 1997.

———. "The Preference for Lengthened Forms in Qumran Hebrew." *Meghillot: Studies in the Dead Sea Scrolls* 1 (2003) 227–40. [Hebrew; English abstract]

Fenton, T. L. "The Claremont 'Mrzḥ' Tablet, Its Text and Meaning." *UF* 9 (1977) 71–75.

Fidler, Ruth. "Qoheleth in 'the House of God': Text and Intertext in Qoh 4:17–5:6 (Eng. 5:1–7)." *HS* 47 (2006) 7–21.

Finkelstein, Louis, ed. *Siphre on Deuteronomy*. Berlin: Jüdischer Kulturbund in Deutschland, 1939. Reprinted, New York: Jewish Theological Seminary, 1969.

Finsterbusch, Karin. "Review of Simone Paganini, '*Nicht darfst du zu diesen Wörtern etwas hinzufügen.*'" *TLZ* 135 (2010) 1101–3.

Fischer, Alexander A. *Skepsis oder Furcht Gottes? Studien zur Komposition und Theologie des Buches Kohelet*. BZAW 247. Berlin: de Gruyter, 1996.

Fishbane, Michael. *Biblical Interpretation in Ancient Israel*. 2nd ed. Oxford: Clarendon, 1988.

Follingstad, Carl M. *Deictic Viewpoint in Biblical Hebrew Text: A Syntagmatic and Paradigmatic Analysis of the Particle כִּי*. Dallas: SIL, 2001.

Fox, Michael. *Ecclesiastes: The Traditional Hebrew Text with the New JPS Translation and Commentary*. Philadelphia: Jewish Publication Society, 2004.

Fraade, Steven D. "Deuteronomy in Sifre to Deuteronomy." Pages 54–59 in vol. 1 of *Encyclopaedia of Midrash: Biblical Interpretation in Formative Judaism*. Edited by Jacob Neusner and Alan J. Avery-Peck. Leiden: Brill, 2005.

_____ . *From Tradition to Commentary: Torah and Its Interpretation in the Midrash Sifre to Deuteronomy*. SUNY Series in Judaica: Hermeneutics, Mysticism, and Religion. Albany: State University of New York, 1991.

Freedman, David Noel, ed. *The Leningrad Codex: A Facsimile Edition*. Grand Rapids, MI: Eerdmans / Leiden: Brill, 1998.

_____ , and Kenneth A. Mathews. *The Paleo-Hebrew Leviticus Scroll (11QpaleoLev)*. Philadelphia: American Schools of Oriental Research, 1985.

Fuller, Russell. "Text-Critical Problems in Malachi 2:10–16." *JBL* 110 (1991) 45–57.

_____ , and Barbara Schlenke. "חטא." Pages 943–50 in vol. 1 of *Theologisches Wörterbuch zu den Qumrantexten*. Stuttgart: Kohlhammer, 2011.

García Martínez, Florentino, Eibert J. C. Tigchelaar, and Adam S. van der Woude. *Manuscripts from Qumran Cave 11 (11Q2–18, 11Q20–31)*. DJD 23. Oxford: Clarendon, 1998.

Gesundheit, Shimon. *Three Times a Year: Studies on the Festival Legislation of the Pentateuch*. FAT 82. Tübingen: Mohr Siebeck, 2012.

Gogel, Sandra L. *A Grammar of Epigraphic Hebrew*. SBLRBS 23. Atlanta: Scholars Press, 1998.

Gordis, Robert. *The Biblical Text in the Making: A Study of the Kethib-Qere*. Augment of 1937 ed. Reprinted, Hoboken, NJ: Ktav, 1971.

_____ . *Koheleth: The Man and His World*. Jewish Theological Seminary of America 19. New York: Bloch, 1955.

Gordon, Cyrus H. "Review of E. Ebeling, *Bruchstücke einer mittelassyrischen Vorschriftensammlung für die Akklimatisierung und Trainierung von Wagenpferden*." *Orientalia* 22 (1953) 231–32.

Graham, William A. "Scripture." Pages 133–45 in vol. 13 of *The Encyclopedia of Religion*. Edited by Mircea Eliade. New York: Macmillan, 1987.

Habel, Norman C. *Literary Criticism of the Old Testament*. Guides to Biblical Scholarship. Philadelphia: Fortress, 1971.

Hammer, Reuven. *Sifre: A Tannaitic Commentary on the Book of Deuteronomy*. Yale Judaica Series 24. New Haven, CT: Yale University Press, 1986.

Hatch, Edwin, and Henry A. Redpath. *A Concordance to the Septuagint and the Other Greek Versions of the Old Testament (Including the Apocryphal Books)*. 2 vols. Oxford: Clarendon, 1897. Suppl., 1906. Reprinted, 2 vols. in 1. Grand Rapids, MI: Baker, 1998.

Hempel, Charlotte. *The Damascus Texts*. Sheffield: Sheffield Academic Press, 2000.

_____ . *The Laws of the Damascus Document: Sources, Tradition and Redaction*. STDJ 29. Leiden: Brill, 1998.

Hoffner, Harry Angier, Jr. *The Laws of the Hittites: A Critical Edition*. DMOA 23. Leiden: Brill, 1997.

Hölscher, Gustav. "Komposition und Ursprung des Deuteronomiums." *ZAW* 40 (1922) 161–255.

Honeyman, A. M. "Varia Punica." *AJP* 68 (1947) 77–82.

Huehnergard, John. *A Grammar of Akkadian*. HSM 45. Atlanta: Scholars Press, 1996. [2nd–3rd eds., Winona Lake, IN: Eisenbrauns, 2005, 2011]

Huwyler, Beat. "'Wenn Gott mit mir ist . . .' (Gen 28,20–22): Zum sprachlichen und theologischen Problem des hebräischen Konditionalsatzes." *TZ* 57 (2001) 10–25.

Jacobs, Louis, and David Derovan. "Hermeneutics." Pages 25–29 in vol. 9 of *Encyclopaedia Judaica*. 22 vols. 2nd ed. Detroit: Macmillan Reference, 2007.

Jassen, Alex P. "American Scholarship on Jewish Law in the Dead Sea Scrolls." Pages 101–54 in *The Dead Sea Scrolls in Scholarly Perspective: A History of Research*. Edited by Devorah Dimant. STDJ 99. Leiden: Brill, 2012.

_____ . *Scripture and Law in the Dead Sea Scrolls and Ancient Judaism*. Cambridge: Cambridge University Press, forthcoming.

Jepsen, Alfred. *Untersuchungen zum Bundesbuch*. BWANT 41. Stuttgart: Kohlhammer, 1927.

Joüon, Paul, and Takamitsu Muraoka. *A Grammar of Biblical Hebrew*. 2 vols. 2nd ed. SubBi 14/1–2. Rome: Pontifical Biblical Institute, 1993.

_____ . *A Grammar of Biblical Hebrew*. 2 vols. in 1. 3rd ed. SubBi 27. Rome: Pontifical Biblical Institute, 2006.

Kaddari, Menachem Z. "The Syntax of כי in the Language of Ben Sira." Pages 87–91 in *The Hebrew of the Dead Sea Scrolls and Ben Sira*. Edited by Takamitsu Muraoka and John F. Elwolde. STDJ 26. Leiden: Brill, 1997.

Kaiser, Otto. "Die Botschaft des Buches Kohelet." *ETL* 71 (1995) 48–70.

Kaufman, Steven A. "The Temple Scroll and Higher Criticism." *HUCA* 53 (1982) 29–43.

Klawans, Jonathan. "The Prohibition of Oaths and Contra-scriptural *Halakhot*: A Response to John P. Meier." *JSHJ* 6 (2008) 33–48.

Knoppers, Gary N., and Bernard M. Levinson. "How, When, Where, and Why Did the Pentateuch Become the Torah." Pages 1–19 in *The Pentateuch as Torah: New Models for Understanding Its Promulgation and Acceptance*. Edited by Gary N. Knoppers and Bernard M. Levinson. Winona Lake, IN: Eisenbrauns, 2007.

Koch, Klaus. "חטא." Pages 858–70 in vol. 2 of *Theologisches Wörterbuch zum Alten Testament*. Edited by G. Johannes Botterweck und Helmer Ringgren. Stuttgart: Kohlhammer, 1977. ET: Pages 309–19 in vol. 4 of *TDOT*. Edited by G. Johannes Botterweck and Helmer Ringgren. Translated by David G. Green. Grand Rapids: Eerdmans, 1980.

Kratz, Reinhard G. *Prophetenstudien: Kleine Schriften II*. FAT 74. Tübingen: Mohr Siebeck, 2011.

Kraus, F. R. "Ein zentrales Problem des altmesopotamischen Rechts: Was ist der Codex Hammurabi." *Genava* 8 (1960) 283–96.

Kropat, Arno. *Die Syntax des Autors der Chronik*. BZAW 16. Gießen: Alfred Töpelmann, 1909.

Krüger, Thomas. *Kohelet (Prediger)*. BKAT 19. Neukirchen-Vluyn: Neukirchener Verlag, 2000.

_____ . *Qoheleth: A Commentary*. Translated by O. C. Dean Jr. Hermeneia. Minneapolis: Fortress, 2004.

_____ . "Die Rezeption der Tora im Buch Kohelet." Pages 303–25 in *Das Buch Kohelet: Studien zur Struktur, Geschichte, Rezeption und Theologie*. Edited by Ludger Schwienhorst-Schönberger. BZAW 254. Berlin: de Gruyter, 1997. Reprinted, pages 173–93, in Krüger, *Kritische Weisheit: Studien zur weisheitlichen Traditionskritik im Alten Testament*. Zurich: Pano, 1997.

Kugel, James L. "Early Jewish Biblical Interpretation." Pages 121–41 in *The Eerdmans Dictionary of Early Judaism*. Edited by John J. Collins and Daniel C. Harlow. Grand Rapids, MI: Eerdmans, 2010.

Kunjummen, Raju D. "The Syntax of Conditionals in Deuteronomy and Translation of *wqatal* [*sic*] (Consecutive Conditionals)." Paper presented at the annual meeting of the SBL. Boston, MA, November 25, 2008. http://www.biblicallaw.net/2008/kunjummen.pdf [accessed 6 June 2011].

Kutscher, Edward Yechezkel. *The Language and Linguistic Background of the Isaiah Scroll (1QIsaᵃ)*. Indices and corrections by Elisha Qimron. 2 vols. STDJ 6–6A. Leiden: Brill, 1974–79.

Landsberger, Benno. "Die Eigenbegrifflichkeit der babylonischen Welt." *Islamica* 2 (1926) 355–72. This essay is reprinted together with "Leitung und Grenze sumerischer und babylonischer Wissenschaft." Edited by Wolfram von Soden. Libelli 142. Darmstadt: Wissenschaftliche Buchgesellschaft, 1965. ET: *The Conceptual Autonomy of the Babylonian World*. Translated by Thorkild Jacobsen, Benjamin R. Foster, and Heinrich von Siebenthal. Introduction by Thorkild Jacobsen. Monographs of the Ancient Near East 1/4. Malibu, CA: Undena, 1976.

Lenhardt, Peter. "Kol Nidrei." Pages 404–5 in *The Oxford Dictionary of the Jewish Religion*. Edited by R. J. Zwi Werblowsky and Geoffrey Wigoder. Oxford: Oxford University Press, 1997.

Levine, Baruch A. *Numbers 21–36: A New Translation with Introduction and Commentary*. AB 4A. New York: Doubleday, 2000.

———. "The Temple Scroll: Aspects of Its Historical Provenance and Literary Character." *BASOR* 232 (1978) 5–23.

Levinson, Bernard M. "The Case for Revision and Interpolation within the Biblical Legal Corpora." Pages 37–59 in *Theory and Method in Biblical and Cuneiform Law: Revision, Interpolation and Development*. Edited by Bernard M. Levinson. JSOTSup 181. Sheffield: Sheffield Academic Press, 1994. Reprinted, pages 201–23 in *"The Right Chorale": Studies in Biblical Law and Interpretation*. FAT 54. Tübingen: Mohr Siebeck, 2008.

———. "Deuteronomy." Pages 356–450 in *The Jewish Study Bible*. Jewish Publication Society *Tanakh* Translation. Oxford: Oxford University Press, 2004.

———. *Deuteronomy and the Hermeneutics of Legal Innovation*. Oxford: Oxford University Press, 1997.

———. "Deuteronomy's Conception of Law as an 'Ideal Type': A Missing Chapter in the History of Constitutional Law." *Judge and Society in Antiquity*. Edited by Aaron Skaist and Bernard M. Levinson. *Maarav: A Journal for the Study of Northwest Semitic Languages and Literatures* 12/1–2 (2005) 83–119. Reprinted, pages 52–86 in *"The Right Chorale": Studies in Biblical Law and Interpretation*. FAT 54. Tübingen: Mohr Siebeck, 2008.

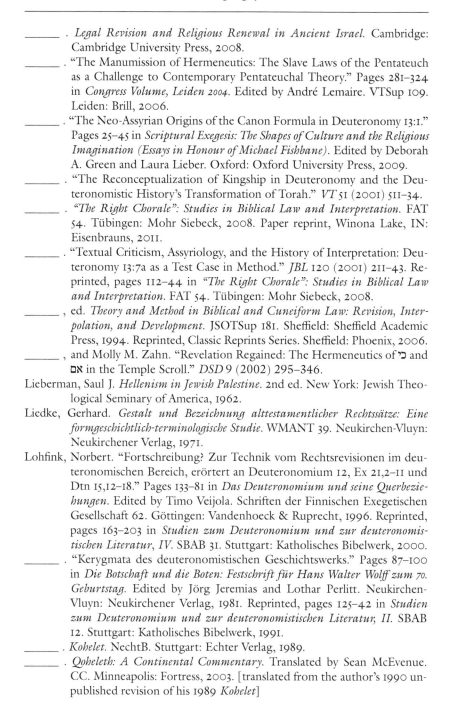

———. *Legal Revision and Religious Renewal in Ancient Israel*. Cambridge: Cambridge University Press, 2008.

———. "The Manumission of Hermeneutics: The Slave Laws of the Pentateuch as a Challenge to Contemporary Pentateuchal Theory." Pages 281–324 in *Congress Volume, Leiden 2004*. Edited by André Lemaire. VTSup 109. Leiden: Brill, 2006.

———. "The Neo-Assyrian Origins of the Canon Formula in Deuteronomy 13:1." Pages 25–45 in *Scriptural Exegesis: The Shapes of Culture and the Religious Imagination (Essays in Honour of Michael Fishbane)*. Edited by Deborah A. Green and Laura Lieber. Oxford: Oxford University Press, 2009.

———. "The Reconceptualization of Kingship in Deuteronomy and the Deuteronomistic History's Transformation of Torah." *VT* 51 (2001) 511–34.

———. *"The Right Chorale": Studies in Biblical Law and Interpretation*. FAT 54. Tübingen: Mohr Siebeck, 2008. Paper reprint, Winona Lake, IN: Eisenbrauns, 2011.

———. "Textual Criticism, Assyriology, and the History of Interpretation: Deuteronomy 13:7a as a Test Case in Method." *JBL* 120 (2001) 211–43. Reprinted, pages 112–44 in *"The Right Chorale": Studies in Biblical Law and Interpretation*. FAT 54. Tübingen: Mohr Siebeck, 2008.

———, ed. *Theory and Method in Biblical and Cuneiform Law: Revision, Interpolation, and Development*. JSOTSup 181. Sheffield: Sheffield Academic Press, 1994. Reprinted, Classic Reprints Series. Sheffield: Phoenix, 2006.

———, and Molly M. Zahn. "Revelation Regained: The Hermeneutics of כי and אם in the Temple Scroll." *DSD* 9 (2002) 295–346.

Lieberman, Saul J. *Hellenism in Jewish Palestine*. 2nd ed. New York: Jewish Theological Seminary of America, 1962.

Liedke, Gerhard. *Gestalt und Bezeichnung alttestamentlicher Rechtssätze: Eine formgeschichtlich-terminologische Studie*. WMANT 39. Neukirchen-Vluyn: Neukirchener Verlag, 1971.

Lohfink, Norbert. "Fortschreibung? Zur Technik vom Rechtsrevisionen im deuteronomischen Bereich, erörtert an Deuteronomium 12, Ex 21,2–11 und Dtn 15,12–18." Pages 133–81 in *Das Deuteronomium und seine Querbeziehungen*. Edited by Timo Veijola. Schriften der Finnischen Exegetischen Gesellschaft 62. Göttingen: Vandenhoeck & Ruprecht, 1996. Reprinted, pages 163–203 in *Studien zum Deuteronomium und zur deuteronomistischen Literatur, IV*. SBAB 31. Stuttgart: Katholisches Bibelwerk, 2000.

———. "Kerygmata des deuteronomistischen Geschichtswerks." Pages 87–100 in *Die Botschaft und die Boten: Festschrift für Hans Walter Wolff zum 70. Geburtstag*. Edited by Jörg Jeremias and Lothar Perlitt. Neukirchen-Vluyn: Neukirchener Verlag, 1981. Reprinted, pages 125–42 in *Studien zum Deuteronomium und zur deuteronomistischen Literatur, II*. SBAB 12. Stuttgart: Katholisches Bibelwerk, 1991.

———. *Kohelet*. NechtB. Stuttgart: Echter Verlag, 1989.

———. *Qoheleth: A Continental Commentary*. Translated by Sean McEvenue. CC. Minneapolis: Fortress, 2003. [translated from the author's 1990 unpublished revision of his 1989 *Kohelet*]

_____ . *Die Väter Israels im Deuteronomium: Mit einer Stellungnahme von Thomas Römer.* OBO 111. Freiburg: Universitätsverlag / Göttingen: Vandenhoeck & Ruprecht, 1991.

_____ . "Warum ist der Tor unfähig, böse zu handeln [Koh 4,17]." Pages 113–20 in *XXI. Deutscher Orientalistentag vom 24. bis 29. März 1980 in Berlin: Ausgewählte Vorträge.* Edited by Fritz Steppat. ZDMGSup 5. Wiesbaden: Steiner, 1983. Reprinted in *Studien zu Kohelet.* SBAB 26. Stuttgart: Katholisches Bibelwerk, 1998.

Mackenzie, Roderick A. F. "The Formal Aspect of Ancient Near Eastern Law." Pages 31–44 in *The Seed of Wisdom: Essays in Honor of T. J. Meek.* Edited by William S. McCullough. Toronto: University of Toronto Press, 1964.

Maier, Johann. *The Temple Scroll: An Introduction, Translation, and Commentary.* Translated by Richard T. White. JSOTSup 34. Sheffield: JSOT Press, 1985.

Marti, Karl. "Das fünfte Buch Mose oder Deuteronomium." Pages 258–327 in *Die Heilige Schrift des Alten Testaments*, vol. 1. Edited by Alfred Bertholet and Emil Kautzsch. 2 vols. 4th ed. Tübingen: Mohr Siebeck, 1922–23.

Mayes, A. D. H. *Deuteronomy.* New Century Bible Commentary. London: Marshall, Morgan & Scott, 1979.

Meier, John P. "Did the Historical Jesus Prohibit All Oaths? Part 1." *JSHJ* 5 (2007) 175–204.

Michel, Diethelm. *Qohelet.* EdF 258. Darmstadt: Wissenschaftliche Buchgesellschaft, 1988.

_____ . "'Unter der Sonne': Zur Immanenz bei Qohelet." Pages 93–111 in *Qohelet in the Context of Wisdom.* Edited by Antoon Schoors. BETL 136. Leuven: Leuven University Press and Peeters, 1998.

Miller, Patrick D. "Prayer and Sacrifice in Ugarit and Israel." Pages 139–55 in *Text and Context: Old Testament and Semitic Studies for F. C. Fensham.* Edited by W. T. Claassen. JSOTSup 48. Sheffield: JSOT Press, 1988. Reprinted, pages 84–100, in Miller, *Israelite Religion and Biblical Theology: Collected Essays.* JSOTSup 267. Sheffield: Sheffield Academic Press, 2000.

Milton, John. *Paradise Lost.* Edited by Alastair Fowler. London: Longman, 1971.

Muilenberg, James. "The Linguistic and Rhetorical Uses of the Particle כי in the Old Testament." *HUCA* 32 (1961) 135–60. Reprinted, pages 208–33 in *Hearing and Speaking the Word: Selections from the Works of James Muilenburg.* Edited by Thomas F. Best. Chico, CA: Scholars Press, 1984.

Muraoka, Takamitsu. "An Approach to the Morphosyntax and Syntax of Qumran Hebrew." Pages 193–214 in *Diggers at the Well: Proceedings of a Third International Symposium on the Hebrew of the Dead Sea Scrolls and Ben Sira.* Edited by Takamitsu Muraoka and John F. Elwolde. STDJ 36. Leiden: Brill, 2000.

_____ . *Emphatic Words and Structures in Biblical Hebrew.* Jerusalem: Magnes / Leiden: Brill, 1985.

_____ . *A Greek-English Lexicon of the Septuagint.* Leuven: Peeters, 2009.

_____ . *Hebrew/Aramaic Index to the Septuagint: Keyed to the Hatch-Redpath Concordance.* Grand Rapids, MI: Baker, 1998.

_____ . "A New Dictionary of Classical Hebrew." Pages 87–101 in *Studies in Ancient Hebrew Semantics*. Edited by Takamitsu Muraoka. AbrNSup 4. Leuven: Peeters, 1995.

Najman, Hindy. "Interpretation as Primordial Writing: Jubilees and Its Authority Conferring Strategies." *JSJ* 30 (1999) 379–410.

_____ . *Seconding Sinai: The Development of Mosaic Discourse in Second Temple Judaism*. JSJSup 77. Leiden: Brill, 2003.

Neudecker, Reinhard. *Moses Interpreted by the Pharisees and Jesus: Matthew's Antitheses in the Light of Early Rabbinic Literature*. SubBi 44. Rome: Gregorian & Biblical Press, 2012.

Nihan, Christophe L. "Review of Reinhard Achenbach, *Die Vollendung der Tora: Studien zur Redaktionsgeschichte des Numeribuches im Kontext von Hexateuch und Pentateuch*." *RBL* 4/2006. http://www. bookreviews.org. [accessed 25 August 2011]

Oesch, Josef M. *Petuchah und Setumah: Untersuchungen zu einer überlieferten Gliederung im hebräischen Text des Alten Testaments*. OBO 27. Göttingen: Vandenhoeck & Ruprecht, 1979.

Osumi, Yuichi. *Die Kompositionsgeschichte des Bundesbuches Exodus 20,22b–23,33*. OBO 105. Freiburg: Universitätsverlag / Göttingen: Vandenhoeck & Ruprecht, 1991.

Otto, Eckart. *Altorientalische und biblische Rechtsgeschichte: Gesammelte Studien*. BZAR 8. Wiesbaden: Harrassowitz, 2008.

_____ . *Das Deuteronomium: Politische Theologie und Rechtsreform in Juda und Assyrien*. BZAW 284. Berlin: de Gruyter, 1999.

_____ . *Korperverletzungen in den Keilschriftrechten und im Alten Testament: Studien zum Rechtstransfer im Alten Orient*. AOAT 226. Kevelaer: Butzon & Bercker / Neukirchen-Vluyn: Neukirchener Verlag, 1991.

_____ . "Die Rechtshermeneutik der Tempelrolle (11QT^a)." *ZABR* 13 (2007) 159–75. Reprinted, pages 547–63 in *Altorientalische und biblische Rechtsgeschichte: Gesammelte Studien*. BZAR 8. Wiesbaden: Harrassowitz, 2008.

_____ . "Die Rechtshermeneutik im Pentateuch und in der Tempelrolle." Pages 72–121 in *Tora in der Hebräischen Bibel: Studien zur Redaktionsgeschichte und synchronen Logik diachroner Transformationen*. Edited by Reinhard Achenbach, Martin Arneth, and Eckart Otto. BZAR 7. Wiesbaden: Harrassowitz, 2007.

_____ . "Temple Scroll and Pentateuch: A Priestly Debate about the Interpretation of the Torah." Pages 59–74 in *The Qumran Legal Texts between the Hebrew Bible and Its Interpretation*. Edited by Kristin De Troyer and Armin Lange. CBET 61. Leuven: Peeters, 2011.

Paganini, Simone. *"Nicht darfst du zu diesen Wörtern etwas hinzufügen": Die Rezeption des Deuteronomiums in der Tempelrolle—Sprache, Autoren und Hermeneutik*. BZAR 11. Wiesbaden: Harrassowitz, 2009.

Paran, Meir. *Forms of the Priestly Style in the Pentateuch: Patterns, Linguistic Usages, Syntactic Structures*. Jerusalem: Magnes, 1989. [Hebrew]

Pardee, Dennis. *Les Textes Hippiatriques: Ras Shamra–Ougarit II*. Paris: Editions Recherche sur les Civilisations, 1985.

_____ . "Ugaritic Science." Pages 223–54 in *The World of the Aramaeans: Studies in Language and Literature in Honour of Paul-Eugène Dion*, vol. 3. Edited by P. M. Michèle Daviau, John W. Wevers, and Michael Weigl. JSOTSup 324–26. Sheffield: Sheffield Academic Press, 2001.

Parker, Simon B. "The Vow in Ugaritic and Israelite Narrative Literature." *Ugarit-Forschungen* 11 (1979) 693–700.

Paul, Shalom M. *Studies in the Book of the Covenant in the Light of Cuneiform and Biblical Law*. VTSup 18. Leiden: Brill, 1970.

Pérez Fernández, Miguel. *An Introductory Grammar of Rabbinic Hebrew*. Translated by John F. Elwolde. Leiden: Brill, 1999.

Peursen, Wido T. van. "Conditional Sentences with אם in the Protasis in Qumran Hebrew." Pages 214–31 in *Diggers at the Well: Proceedings of a Third International Symposium on the Hebrew of the Dead Sea Scrolls and Ben Sira*. Edited by Takamitsu Muraoka and John F. Elwolde. STDJ 36. Leiden: Brill, 2000.

Puech, Émile. "Fragments du plus ancien exemplaire du Roleau du Temple (4Q524)." Pages 19–52 in *Legal Texts and Legal Issues: Proceedings of the Second Meeting of the International Organization for Qumran Studies*. Edited by Moshe J. Bernstein, Florentino García Martínez, and John Kampen. STDJ 23. Leiden: Brill, 1997.

_____ . *Textes Hébreux (4Q521–528, 4Q576–579): Qumran Cave 4.XVIII*. DJD 25. Oxford: Clarendon, 1997.

Qimron, Elisha. מגילות מדבר יהודה: החיבורים העבריים. (*The Dead Sea Scrolls: The Hebrew Writings*, vol. 1. *Between Bible and Mishnah*.) 3 vols. Jerusalem: Yad Ben-Zvi, 2010. [Hebrew; English introduction]

_____ . *The Hebrew of the Dead Sea Scrolls*. HSS 29. Atlanta: Scholars Press, 1986.

_____ . *The Temple Scroll: A Critical Edition with Extensive Reconstructions*. Bibliography by Florentino García Martínez. Judean Desert Studies 131. Beer Sheva: Ben-Gurion University of the Negev Press / Jerusalem: Israel Exploration Society, 1996.

_____ , and John Strugnell. *Qumran Cave 4.V: Miqṣat Maʿaśe ha-Torah*. DJD 10. Oxford: Clarendon, 1994.

Reventlow, Henning Graf. *Das Heiligkeitsgesetz: Formgeschichtlich untersucht*. WMANT 6. Neukirchen-Vluyn: Neukirchener Verlag, 1961.

Rey, Jean-Sébastien. "Quelques particularités linguistiques communes à 4QInstruction et à Ben Sira." Pages 155–74 in *Conservatism and Innovation in the Hebrew Language of the Hellenistic Period: Proceedings of a Fourth International Symposium on the Hebrew of the Dead Sea Scrolls and Ben Sira*. Edited by Jan Joosten and Jean-Sébastien Rey. STDJ 73. Leiden: Brill, 2008.

Riska, Magnus. *The House of the Lord: A Study of the Temple Scroll, Columns 29:3b–47:18*. Publications of the Finnish Exegetical Society 93. Helsinki: Finnish Exegetical Society / Göttingen: Vandenhoeck & Ruprecht, 2007.

_____ . *The Temple Scroll and the Biblical Text Traditions: A Study of Columns 2–13:9*. Publications of the Finnish Exegetical Society 81. Helsinki: Finnish Exegetical Society, 2001.

Rofé, Alexander. "The 'Angel' in Qoh 5:5 in Light of a Wisdom Discussion Formula." *ErIsr* 14 (Ginsberg Volume; 1978) 105–9. [Hebrew]

—————. *Introduction to Deuteronomy: Part I and Further Chapters.* Jerusalem: Akademon, 1988. [Hebrew]

—————. "The Wisdom Formula 'Do Not Say . . .' and the Angel in Qoh 5:5." Pages 364–76 in *Reading from Right to Left: Essays on the Hebrew Bible in Honour of David J. A. Clines.* Edited by J. Cheryl Exum and H. G. M. Williamson. Sheffield: Sheffield Academic Press, 2003.

Römer, Thomas. *Israels Väter: Untersuchungen zur Väterthematik im Deuteronomium und in der deuteronomistischen Tradition.* OBO 99. Freiburg: Universitätsverlag / Göttingen: Vandenhoeck & Ruprecht, 1990.

Roth, Martha T. *Law Collections from Mesopotamia and Asia Minor.* 2nd ed. SBLWAW 6. Atlanta: Scholars Press, 1997.

Rudolph, Wilhelm. *Vom Buch Kohelet: Vortrag, gehalten anlässlich des Rektoratsantritts am 12. November 1958.* Münster: Aschendorff, 1959.

Rüterswörden, Udo. "Die Apodosis in den Rechtssätzen des Deuteronomiums." *ZAH* 15/16 (2002–3) 124–37.

Sauer, Georg. *Unterweisungen in lehrhafter Form: Jesus Sirach (Ben Sira).* JSHRZ 3. Gütersloh: Mohn, 1981.

Schiffman, Lawrence H. "The Deuteronomic Paraphrase of the Temple Scroll." *RevQ* 15 (1992) 543–67. Reprinted, pages 443–70 in *The Courtyards of the House of the Lord: Studies on the Temple Scroll.* Edited by Florentino García Martínez. STDJ 75. Leiden: Brill, 2008.

—————. "Halakhic Elements in the Sapiential Texts from Qumran." Pages 89–100 in *Sapiential Perspectives: Wisdom Literature in Light of the Dead Sea Scrolls: Proceedings of the Sixth International Symposium of the Orion Center for the Study of the Dead Sea Scrolls and Associated Literature, 20–22 May, 2001.* Edited by John J. Collins, Gregory E. Sterling, and Ruth A. Clements. STDJ 51. Leiden: Brill, 2004. Reprinted under new title as "Halakhic Elements in 4QInstruction," pages 204–15 in *Qumran and Jerusalem: Studies in the Dead Sea Scrolls and the History of Judaism.* Studies in the Dead Sea Scrolls and Related Literature. Grand Rapids, MI: Eerdmans, 2010.

—————. "The Laws of Vows and Oaths (Num. 30, 3–16) in the Zadokite Fragments and the Temple Scroll." *RevQ* 15 (1991) 199–214. Reprinted, pages 557–72 in *The Courtyards of the House of the Lord: Studies on the Temple Scroll.* Edited by Florentino García Martínez. STDJ 75. Leiden: Brill, 2008.

—————. "The Temple Scroll and the Halakhic Pseudepigrapha of the Second Temple Period." Pages 121–31 in *Pseudepigraphic Perspectives: The Apocrypha and Pseudepigrapha in Light of the Dead Sea Scrolls.* Edited by Esther G. Chazon and Michael Stone. STDJ 31. Leiden: Brill, 1999. Reprinted, pages 163–74 in *The Courtyards of the House of the Lord: Studies on the Temple Scroll.* Edited by Florentino García Martínez. STDJ 75. Leiden: Brill, 2008.

_____ , with James H. Charlesworth et al. *The Dead Sea Scrolls: Hebrew, Aramaic, and Greek Texts with English Translations*, vol. 7: *Temple Scroll and Related Documents.* Princeton Theological Seminary Dead Sea Scrolls Project. Tübingen: Mohr Siebeck / Louisville: Westminster John Knox, 2011.

Schniedewind, William M. "Linguistic Ideology in Qumran Hebrew." Pages 245–55 in *Diggers at the Well: Proceedings of a Third International Symposium on the Hebrew of the Dead Sea Scrolls and Ben Sira.* Edited by Takamitsu Muraoka and John F. Elwolde. STDJ 36. Leiden: Brill, 2000.

_____ . "Qumran Hebrew as an Anti-language." *JBL* 118 (1999) 235–52.

Schoors, Antoon. "Introduction." Pages 1–13 in *Qohelet in the Context of Wisdom.* Edited by Antoon Schoors. BETL 136. Leuven: Leuven University Press and Peeters, 1998.

_____ . "The Particle כי." Pages 240–76 in *Remembering All the Way . . . : A Collection of Old Testament Studies Published on the Occasion of the Fortieth Anniversary of the Oudtestamentisch Werkgezelschap in Nederland.* Edited by Bertil Albrektson et al. OtSt 21. Leiden: Brill, 1981.

_____ . *The Preacher Sought to Find Pleasing Words: A Study of the Language of Qoheleth.* OLA 41. Leuven: Peeters & Department of Oriental Studies, 1992.

_____ . *The Preacher Sought to Find Pleasing Words: A Study of the Language of Qoheleth, Part II: Vocabulary.* OLA 143. Leuven: Peeters & Department of Oriental Studies, 2004.

Schüle, Andreas. *Die Syntax der althebräischen Inschriften: Ein Beitrag zur historischen Grammatik des Hebräischen.* AOAT 270. Münster: Ugarit-Verlag, 2000.

Schwienhorst-Schönberger, Ludger. *Kohelet.* Herders Theologischer Kommentar zum Alten Testament. Freiburg: Herder, 2004.

_____ , ed. *Das Buch Kohelet: Studien zur Struktur, Geschichte, Rezeption und Theologie.* BZAW 254. Berlin: de Gruyter, 1997.

Seebass, Horst. "Eid II. Altes Testament." Pages 376–77 in vol. 9 of *Theologische Realenzyklopädie.* Edited by Gerhard Müller. Berlin: de Gruyter, 1982.

_____ . *Numeri: Kapitel 22,2–36,13.* BKAT 4/3. Neukirchen-Vluyn: Neukirchener Verlag, 2007.

Segal, M. H. *A Grammar of Mishnaic Hebrew.* Oxford: Clarendon, 1927.

Segert, Stanislav. "Form and Function of Ancient Israelite, Greek and Roman Legal Sentences." Pages 151–59 in *Orient and Occident: Essays Presented to Cyrus H. Gordon on the Occasion of His Sixty-Fifth Birthday.* Edited by Harry A. Hoffner. AOAT 22. Kevelaer: Butzon & Bercker / Neukirchen-Vluyn: Neukirchener Verlag, 1973.

Seitz, Gottfried. *Redaktionsgeschichtliche Studien zum Deuteronomium.* BWANT 93. Stuttgart: Kohlhammer, 1971.

Seow, C. L. *Ecclesiastes: A New Translation with Introduction and Commentary.* AB 18C. New York: Doubleday, 1997.

_____ . "Linguistic Evidence and the Dating of Qohelet." *JBL* 115 (1996) 643–66.

Shemesh, Aharon. "'Three Days' Journey from the Temple': The Use of This Expression in the Temple Scroll." *DSD* 6 (1999) 126–38.

Shinan, Avigdor. *Midrash Shemot Rabbah, Chapters I–XIV: A Critical Edition Based on a Jerusalem Manuscript with Variants, Commentary, and Introduction.* Jerusalem: Dvir, 1984. [Hebrew]

Shulman, Ahouva. "The Function of the 'Jussive' and 'Indicative' Imperfect Forms in Biblical Hebrew Prose." *ZAH* 13 (2000) 168–80.

Skehan, Patrick W., and Alexander A. DiLella. *The Wisdom of Ben Sira.* AB 39. New York: Doubleday, 1987.

Skehan, Patrick W., Eugene Ulrich, and Judith E. Sanderson. *Qumran Cave 4.IV: Palaeo-Hebrew and Greek Biblical Manuscripts.* DJD 9. Oxford: Clarendon, 1992.

Smith, George Adam. *The Book of Deuteronomy: In the Revised Version with Introduction and Notes.* Cambridge Bible for Schools and Colleges. Cambridge: Cambridge University Press, 1918.

Soden, Wolfram von, with Werner R. Mayer. *Grundriss der Akkadischen Grammatik.* 3rd ed. AnOr 33. Rome: Pontifical Biblical Institute, 1995.

Spangenberg, Izak J. J. "A Century of Wrestling with Qohelet: The Research History of the Book Illustrated with a Discussion of Qoh 4,17–5,6." Pages 61–91 in *Qohelet in the Context of Wisdom.* Edited by Antoon Schoors. BETL 136. Leuven: Leuven University Press and Peeters, 1998.

Stackert, Jeffrey. *Rewriting the Torah: Literary Revision in Deuteronomy and the Holiness Legislation.* FAT 52. Tübingen: Mohr Siebeck, 2007.

Stegemann, Hartmut, Eileen Schuller, and Carol Newsom. *1QHodayot*ᵃ*, with Incorporation of 1QHodayot*ᵇ *and 4QHodayot*ᵃ⁻ᶠ. DJD 40. Oxford: Clarendon, 2009.

Steuernagel, Carl. *Das Deuteronomium übersetzt und erklärt.* Göttinger Handkommentar zum Alten Testament. Göttingen: Vandenhoeck & Ruprecht, 1899.

———. *Übersetzung und Erklärung der Bücher Deuteronomium und Josua und allgemeine Einleitung in den Hexateuch.* HKAT. Göttingen: Vandenhoeck & Ruprecht, 1900.

Strugnell, John, Daniel J. Harrington, and Torleif Elgvin, in consultation with Joseph A. Fitzmyer. *Sapiential Texts, Part 2: Cave 4.XXIV.* DJD 34. Oxford: Clarendon, 1999.

Tal, Abraham, and Moshe Florentin. *The Pentateuch: The Samaritan Version and the Masoretic Version.* Tel Aviv: Haim Rubin Tel Aviv University Press, 2010.

Talmon, Shemaryahu. "Aspects of the Textual Transmission of the Bible in the Light of Qumran Manuscripts." *Textus* 4 (1964) 95–132. Reprinted, pages 226–63 in *Qumran and the History of the Biblical Text.* Edited by Frank Moore Cross and Shemaryahu Talmon. Cambridge: Harvard University Press, 1975.

———. "Double Readings in the Massoretic Text." *Textus* 1 (1960) 144–84. Reprinted, pages 217–66 in *Text and Canon of the Hebrew Bible: Collected Studies.* Winona Lake, IN: Eisenbrauns, 2010.

_____ . "Synonymous Readings in the Textual Traditions of the Old Testament." Pages 335–83 in *Studies in the Bible*. Edited by Chaim Rabin. ScrHier 8. Jerusalem: Magnes, 1961. Reprinted with new title as "Synonymous Readings in the Masoretic Text," pages 171–216 in *Text and Canon of the Hebrew Bible: Collected Studies*. Winona Lake, IN: Eisenbrauns, 2010.

_____ , and Yigael Yadin. *Masada VI: Yigael Yadin Excavations 1963–1965: Final Reports*. Jerusalem: Israel Exploration Society and Hebrew University of Jerusalem, 1999.

Tanakh: The Holy Scriptures. The New JPS Translation according to the Traditional Hebrew Text. Philadelphia: Jewish Publication Society, 1988.

Taradach, Madeleine, and Joan Ferrer. *Un Targum de Qohélet: Ms. M-2 de Salamanca, Editio princeps—Texte araméen, traduction et commentaire critique*. MdB 37. Geneva: Labor et Fides, 1998.

Thorion, Yohanan. "Die Sprache der Tempelrolle und die Chronikbücher." *RevQ* 11 (1982–84) 423–26.

_____ . *Studien zur klassischen hebräischen Syntax*. Marburger Studien zur Afrika- und Asienkunde B/6. Berlin: Reimer, 1984.

Thuesen, Peter J. *In Discordance with the Scriptures: American Protestant Battles over Translating the Bible*. Oxford: Oxford University Press, 1999.

Tigay, Jeffery H. *Deuteronomy: The JPS Torah Commentary*. Philadelphia: Jewish Publication Society, 1996.

Tita, Hubert. *Gelübde als Bekenntnis: Eine Studie zu den Gelübden im Alten Testament*. OBO 181. Freiburg: Universitätsverlag / Göttingen: Vandenhoeck & Ruprecht, 2001.

Tjen, Anwar. *On Conditionals in the Greek Pentateuch: A Study of Translation Syntax*. Library of Hebrew Bible/Old Testament Studies 515. New York; London: T. & T. Clark, 2010.

Tov, Emanuel. "Appendix F: Texts from the Judean Desert." Pages 176–233 in *The SBL Handbook of Style for Ancient Near Eastern, Biblical, and Early Christian Studies*. Peabody, MA: Hendrickson, 1999.

_____ . "The Authority of Early Hebrew Scripture Texts." *Journal of Reformed Theology* 5 (2011) 276–95.

_____ . "The Background of the Sense Divisions in the Biblical Texts." Pages 334–35 in *Delimitation Criticism: A New Tool in Biblical Scholarship*. Edited by Marjo C. A. Korpel and Josef M. Oesch. Pericope 1. Assen: Van Gorcum, 2000.

_____ . "Deut. 12 and 11QTemple LII–LIII: A Contrastive Analysis." *RevQ* 15 (1991) 169–73.

_____ . "The Discoveries in the Judaean Desert Series: History and System of Presentation." Pages 1–25 in *The Texts from the Judaean Desert: Indices and an Introduction to the Discoveries in the Judaean Desert Series*. Edited by Emanuel Tov, with contributions by Martin Abegg, Jr. et al. DJD 39. Oxford: Clarendon, 2002.

_____ . "Glosses, Interpolations, and Other Types of Scribal Additions in the Text of the Hebrew Bible." In *Language, Theology, and the Bible: Essays in Honour of James Barr*. Edited by Samuel E. Balentine and John Barton. Oxford: Clarendon, 1994. Reprinted, pages 53–74 in Tov, *The Greek and Hebrew Bible: Collected Essays on the Septuagint*. VTSup 72. Leiden: Brill, 1999.

_____. "Hebrew Biblical Manuscripts from the Judean Desert: Their Contribution to Textual Criticism." *JJS* 39 (1988) 5–37.

_____. "The Orthography and Language of the Hebrew Scrolls Found at Qumran and the Origin of These Scrolls." *Textus* 13 (1986) 31–37.

_____. "Provisional List of Documents from the Judean Desert." In *Encyclopedia of the Dead Sea Scrolls*. Edited by Lawrence H. Schiffman and James C. VanderKam. 2 vols. Oxford: Oxford University Press, 2000.

_____. *Textual Criticism of the Hebrew Bible*. 3rd rev. ed. Minneapolis: Fortress, 2012.

Tropper, Josef. *Ugaritische Grammatik*. AOAT 273. Münster: Ugarit-Verlag, 2000.

Ulrich, Eugene, and Frank Moore Cross. *Qumran Cave 4.VII: Genesis to Numbers*. DJD 12. Oxford: Clarendon, 1994.

Ulrich, Eugene, Frank Moore Cross, Sidnie White Crawford, Julie Ann Duncan, Patrick W. Skehan, Emanuel Tov, and Julio Trebolle Barrera. *Qumran Cave 4.IX: Deuteronomy to Kings*. DJD 14. Oxford: Clarendon, 1995.

VanderKam, James C. "Moses Trumping Moses: Making the Book of *Jubilees*." Pages 25–44 in *The Dead Sea Scrolls: Transmission of Traditions and Production of Texts*. Edited by Sarianna Metso, Hindy Najman, and Eileen Schuller. STDJ 92. Leiden: Brill, 2010.

_____. "Questions of Canon Viewed through the Dead Sea Scrolls." *Bulletin for Biblical Research* 11 (2001) 269–92.

_____. "The Temple Scroll and the Book of Jubilees." Pages 211–36 in *Temple Scroll Studies: Papers Presented at the International Symposium on the Temple Scroll, Manchester, December 1987*. Edited by George J. Brooke. Journal for the Study of the Pseudepigrapha Supplement 7. Sheffield: Sheffield Academic Press, 1989.

Waltke, Bruce K., and Michael Patrick O'Connor. *An Introduction to Biblical Hebrew Syntax*. Winona Lake, IN: Eisenbrauns, 1990.

Weinfeld, Moshe. *Deuteronomy and the Deuteronomic School*. Oxford: Clarendon, 1972. Reprinted, Winona Lake, IN: Eisenbrauns, 1992.

_____. "God versus Moses in the Temple Scroll: 'I Do Not Speak on My Own but on God's Authority' (Sifrei Deut. Sec. 5; John 12,48f)." *RevQ* 15 (1991) 175–80.

Weissenberg, Hanne von, Juha Pakkala, and Marko Marttila, eds. *Changes in Scripture: Rewriting and Interpreting Authoritative Traditions in the Second Temple Period*. Berlin: de Gruyter, 2011.

Weitzman, Steve. "Why Did the Qumran Community Write in Hebrew?" *JAOS* 119 (1999) 35–45.

Wevers, John William. *Notes on the Greek Text of Deuteronomy*. SBLSCS 39. Atlanta: Scholars Press, 1995.

White, Sidnie. *See* Crawford, Sidnie White.

Williams, Ronald J. *Hebrew Syntax: An Outline*. 2nd ed. Toronto: University of Toronto Press, 1976. Revised and expanded by John C. Beckman, *Wil-*

liams' *Hebrew Syntax.* 3rd ed. Toronto: University of Toronto Press, 2007.

Wilson, Andrew M., and Lawrence Wills. "Literary Sources of the Temple Scroll." *HTR* 75 (1982) 275–88.

Wise, Michael O. *A Critical Study of the Temple Scroll from Qumran Cave 11.* SAOC 49. Chicago: University of Chicago Press, 1990.

Wright, David P. *Inventing God's Law: How the Covenant Code of the Bible Used and Revised the Laws of Hammurabi.* Oxford: Oxford University Press, 2009.

Würthwein, Ernst. *The Text of the Old Testament.* Translated from 4th German ed. Grand Rapids, MI: Eerdmans, 1979.

Yadin, Yigael. *Tefillin from Qumran.* Jerusalem: Israel Exploration Society and the Shrine of the Book, 1969.

_____. מגילת המקדש. (*The Temple Scroll.*) 4 vols. Jerusalem: Israel Exploration Society, 1977. Translated as *The Temple Scroll.* 3 vols. Jerusalem: Israel Exploration Society, 1977–83.

Yeivin, Israel. *Introduction to the Tiberian Masorah.* SBLMasS 5. Chico, CA: Scholars Press, 1979.

Zahn, Molly M. "4QReworked Pentateuch C and the Literary Sources of the *Temple Scroll*: A New (Old) Proposal." *DSD* 19 (2012) 133–58.

_____. "Get Fuzzy: The Elusive Rewriters of Scripture." ASOR Blog. September 2012. http://asorblog.org/?p=3173#more-317. [accessed 5 May 2013]

_____. "Identifying Reuse of Scripture in the Temple Scroll: Some Methodological Reflections." Pages 341–58 in *A Teacher for All Generations: Essays in Honor of James C. VanderKam*, vol. 1. Edited by Eric F. Mason, Samuel I. Thomas, Alison Schofield, and Eugene Ulrich. 2 vols. JSJSup 153. Leiden: Brill, 2012.

_____. "New Voices, Ancient Words: The *Temple Scroll*'s Reuse of the Bible." Pages 435–58 in *Temple and Worship in Biblical Israel: Proceedings of the Oxford Old Testament Seminar.* JSOTSup 422. London: T. & T. Clark, 2007.

_____. "Reexamining Empirical Models: The Case of Exodus 13." Pages 36–55 in *Das Deuteronomium zwischen Pentateuch und deuteronomistischem Geschichtswerk.* FRLANT 206. Göttingen: Vandenhoeck & Ruprecht, 2004.

_____. *Rethinking Rewritten Scripture: Composition and Exegesis in the 4QReworked Pentateuch Manuscripts.* STDJ 95. Leiden: Brill, 2011.

_____. "Review of Eckart Otto, *Altorientalische und biblische Rechtsgeschichte: Gesammelte Studien.*" *JAOS* 132 (2012) 128–29.

_____. "Review of Reinhard Achenbach, Martin Arneth, and Eckart Otto, *Tora in der Hebräischen Bibel: Studien zur Redaktionsgeschichte und synchronen Logik diachroner Transformationen.*" *JAOS* 129 (2009) 329–30.

_____. "Review of Simone Paganini, '*Nicht darfst du zu diesen Wörtern etwas hinzufügen.*'" *JHS* 10 (2010). http://www.arts.ualberta.ca/JHS/reviews/reviews_new/review450.htm [accessed 25 August 2011]. Reprinted, pages 616–19 in *Perspectives on Hebrew Scriptures VII: Comprising the*

Contents of Journal of Hebrew Scriptures, vol. 10. Edited by Ehud Ben Zvi. Perspectives on Hebrew Scriptures and Its Contexts 15. Piscataway, NJ: Gorgias, 2011.

_____. "Schneiderei oder Weberei: Zum Verständnis der Diachronie der Tempelrolle." *RevQ* 20 (2001) 255–86.

Index of Authors

Index of Scripture

New Testament and Apocrypha

Index of Other Ancient Sources

Note: Not included here are sources found in the appendixes, which are organized clearly by text (see pp. 95–109).

Texts from the Judean Desert

Ancient Near Eastern, Classical, and Rabbinic Sources

Index of Subjects